Shape-shifters and their Stories

Michael Berman

Mandrake

Published by
Mandrake of Oxford
PO Box 250
OXFORD
OX1 1AP (UK)

Also by Michael Berman and published by Mandrake
Sacred Mountains: Stories of the Mystic Mountains

"Long ago the trees thought they were really people
Long ago the mountains thought they were really people
Long ago the animals thought they were really people
Someday, they will say
Long ago the humans thought they were really people"
Constance O'Day-Flannery, *Shifting Love*

Contents

Introduction

Shape-shifting is a common theme in mythology, folklore, and fairy tales. In its broadest sense, shape-shifting occurs when a being (usually human) either (1) has the ability to change its shape into that of another person, creature, or other entity or (2) finds its shape involuntarily changed by someone else. If the shape change is voluntary, its cause may be an act of will, a magic word or magic words, a potion, or a magic object. If the change is involuntary, its cause may be a curse or spell, a wizard's or magician's or fairy's help, a deity's will, a temporal change such as a full Moon or nightfall, love, or death. The transformation may or may not be purposeful.

The desire to be different in some way so as to match some ideal promoted through advertising has become an obsession, especially for vulnerable younger members of society. Perhaps the pressure to conform to some unrealistic ideal is something that has always been with us, but surely not to the extent that now is the case. And it is this desire that helps to account for the current interest in shape-shifting as it would seem to provide a means of achieving the goal to bring about change. However, as many of the tales in this collection show, it is only by coming to terms with who we really are that peace of mind can truly be ours once again.

Another, and perhaps even more significant reason for the fascination with shape-shifting is that stories and shamanic journeys that involve such transformations let us cross the threshold between this reality and other worlds, at least in imagination. Through such tales and journeys we learn to appreciate that we can in fact wear many shapes and inhabit many skins, and we are reminded that we are all living beings beneath the fur, the feathers, and the scales.

Having no scripture, liturgy or singular deity, if one's … desire is to find universal truth it is easy to perceive the Pagan outlook as too diverse and individualistic to have any weight or worth. (Restall Orr, 2012, p.96).

On the other hand, if you take a Bible and put it out in the wind and rain, soon the paper on which the words are printed will disintegrate and the words will be gone, whereas for the Pagan his or her Bible IS the wind and rain. And although there may not necessarily be key texts or set teachings to guide the Pagan, there are stories: legends shared with other people, other lands, tales from other, older, cultures that speak to us, and it is those stories that form the focus of this book.

Reference

'Pagan Ecology: on our perception of nature, ancestry and home' by Emma Restall Orr. In MacLellan, G. & Cross, S. (2012) *The Wanton Green*, Mandrake of Oxford.

A Shape-shifter
from Svaneti

Shape-shifting occurs when a being (usually human) either has the ability to change its shape into that of another person, creature, or other entity or finds its shape involuntarily changed by someone else.

One of the attributes often credited to shamans, as well as to witches and other kinds of magical practitioner, is the ability to shape-shift from human into animal shape. Sometimes this change is a literal one, human flesh transformed into animal flesh or covered over by animal skin; in other accounts, the soul leaves the shaman's unconscious body to enter into the body of an animal, fish or bird. And it is not only shamans who have such powers according to tales from around the globe. Shape shifting is part of a mythic and story-telling tradition stretching back over thousands of years. The Gods of various mythologies are credited with this ability, as are the heroes of the great epic sagas.

In Nordic myth, Odin could change his shape into any beast or bird; in Greek myth, Zeus often assumed animal shape in his relentless pursuit of young women. Cernunnos, the lord of animals in Celtic mythology, wore the shape of a stag, and also the shape of a man with a heavy rack of horns. In the *Odyssey*, Homer tells the tale of Proteus—a famous soothsayer who would not give away his knowledge unless forced to do so. Menelaus came upon him while he slept, and held on to him tightly as he shape-shifted into a lion, a snake, a leopard, a bear, etc. Defeated, Proteus returned to his own shape and Menelaus won the answers to his questions.

[The story of Proteus in Homer's *Odyssey* is echoed in the magical

Celtic tale of the resourceful Gwion Bach — a young man who went on to become the great Welsh poet Taliesin. Gwion Bach stole the gift of prophesy from the cauldron of the witch Ceridwen — and then he fled, with the furious old witch in hot pursuit. He transformed himself into a hare; the witch transformed into a hound. He turned into a fish, she turned into an otter, etc., etc., until Gwion Bach eventually became a grain of wheat. The witch became a hen, gobbled him up, and gave birth to him (as the infant Taliesin) nine months later. In the ballad *Tam Lin*, the hero undergoes a Protean series of transformations too: he becomes a bear, a poisonous snake, and a red-hot brand of iron, but his lady love bravely stands her ground and holds on to him somehow. And when Tam Lin regains his own true shape, she's won him from the Queen of Faery.]

Not all transformations are from human to animal shape. The Great Silkie of Sule Skerry described in Scottish ballads, is a man upon dry land, a silkie [seal] in the sea, and he leaves a human maid pregnant with his child. And Irish legends tell of men who marry seal or otter women and then hide their animal skins from them to prevent them from returning to the water. Generally these women bear several sons, but pine away for their true home. If they manage to find the skin, they then return to the sea with barely a thought for the ones left behind.

Japanese fairy tales warn of the danger of kitsune, the fox-wife. The fox takes on the form of a beautiful woman in these stories, but to wed her brings madness and death. In Tibet, a frog-husband is an unexpected source of joy to a shy young bride. He is not a man disguised as a frog but a frog disguised as a man. When his young wife burns his frog skin to keep her lover in the shape she prefers, the frog-husband loses his magical powers, gracefully resigning himself to ordinary human life instead (Berman, 2007, pp.134-135).

We all go through a stage in life of wanting, and often even trying, to be what we are not, hence the fascination with shape-shifting all through the ages. In my own case, for example, born with curly hair, I spent hours blow-drying it in my teenage years to make it look straight, and then of course there are those born with curly hair who long to make it straight. Whether it is a wish for breast enlargements or reductions, injections of Botox or liposuction, hair transplants or depilation - the list is endless. Then there are those who seek more fundamental changes, gender reassignment for example.

This yearning in our formative years for changes to the "script" that were never intended seems to be more or less universal, that is until we finally learn to come to terms with who we are, and this that helps to explain our fascination with the theme.

The Chosen One is a folktale from Svanetia, translated from Georgian into English by Ketevan Kalandadze. It is a story about an only son who undergoes a form of initiation, during which a shape-shifting contest takes place that leads to him becoming a man.

Situated on the southern slopes of the central Greater Caucasus, the province of Svaneti (Georgian: სვანეთი) is in the north western part of Georgia. The landscape is dominated by mountains that are separated by deep gorges, and four of the 10 highest peaks of the Caucasus are located in the region. The highest mountain in Georgia, Mount Shkhara at 5,201 meters (17,059 feet), is also to be found in the province.

The Svans, the indigenous population of Svaneti, were Christianized in the 4th-6th centuries. However, some remnants of old Paganism have also been maintained in the region, and this particular tale most probably dates back to the pre-Christian times.

The Chosen One

There was an old couple. They had an only son who had special powers and could see into the future. One day the father took his son with him when he went to the forest to gather some firewood. And this is what his son said to him there:

> "A red man will come here to take me away from you today but, before he comes, I'll turn into a red horse. However much money he offers you, on no account must you sell me to him!"

He finished his words and, just as he said he would, turned into a red horse. Soon after that, the red man turned up. When he saw the red horse he asked the old man to sell it to him. At first the old man refused, just as he had been told to do. But the red man was very persuasive, bargained hard with him, and the old man finally agreed. The red man then saddled the horse and, with a golden halter, took him home. The red man grew to love his horse so much that he wouldn't trust anyone to care for it. When he had to go out, nobody was allowed to exercise the horse in his place, and the instructions were to give it water to drink in its stable.

But one day the red man was away and his children took the horse to water. The red horse had been waiting for this moment, and used it as an opportunity to escape. As soon as he tried to run away though, the red man reappeared. The horse turned into a trout and jumped into the water, but the red man turned into a swan and dived into the water to catch it. The trout then turned into an apple and dropped into the lap of a real mzetunakhavi (beauty), but the red man turned into a small knife and landed in her lap too. The mzetunakhavi took the knife and was about to cut the apple when the apple turned into a needle. The knife turned into a thread and passed through the eye of the needle. The boy had been waiting for that moment and took the opportunity to jump into the fire. The thread burnt but the needle was undamaged, and turned into a young man again.

"You saved me today," the young man said to the mzetunakhavi. "And I'm not going anywhere. Be my wife and let me be your husband!"

The mzetunakhavi really liked the young man and so she accepted his proposal. They had their wedding in the mzetunakhavi's kingdom, and then continued the partying at the house of the young man's parents.

Reference:

Berman, M. (2007) *The Nature of Shamanism and the Shamanic Story*, Newcastle: Cambridge Scholars Publishing.

John William Waterhouse, Mermaid

The Great Silkie
of Sule Skerry:
Shape-shifter & Diviner

In The Great Selkie of Sule Skerry, a ballad from Orkney, a woman longs to know who exactly her son's father is. A man appears and admits to being the father but informs her that he is a selkie: a man only on the land, a seal in the water. He takes his son, gives her a purse of gold, and predicts that she will marry a gunner, who will shoot both him and their son.

Silkie is simply the Orcadian dialect word for "seal", and silkies are a very common sight across Orkney. A common element in all the silkie folk-tales is the fact that in order to shape-shift, they have to cast off their sealskins. Within these magical skins lay the power to return to seal form, and therefore the sea. If this sealskin was lost, or stolen, the creature was doomed to remain in human form until it could be recovered.

The Waters have been described as the reservoir of all the potentialities of existence because they not only precede every form but they also serve to sustain every creation. Immersion is equivalent to dissolution of form, in other words death, whereas emergence repeats the cosmogonic act of formal manifestation, in other words rebirth (see Eliade, 1952, p.151). And, following on from this, the surface of water can be defined as "the meeting place and doorway from one realm to another: from that which is revealed to that which is hidden, from conscious to unconscious" (Shaw & Francis, 2008, p.13). And for these reasons it provides the ideal medium for the transformation of the seal into a man and then back into silkie form again.

A silkie-man in human form was said to be a handsome creature, with almost magical seductive powers over mortal women. And should a mortal woman wish to make contact with a silkie-man, there was a specific rite she had to follow. At high tide, she had to make her way to the shore and shed seven tears into the sea. The silkie-man would then come ashore for her.

The Great Silkie of Sule Skerry
In Norwa' land there lived a maid
'Ba! Luly [fair/pale] wean [child]! This maid she sang,
'Sin' little ken [know] I my bairn's [child's] father,
Far less the land where he bides in!
And he come ae [one] night to her bed foot,
And a grumly [fierce/grim] guest I'm sure was he,
Saying, 'Here am I, thy bairn's father,
Although I may no' comely be.
I am a man upon the land,
I am a silkie [seal] on the sea;
And when I'm far and far frae [from] land,
My home it is in Sule Skerry.'
And he has ta'en a purse of gold,
And he has placed it on her knee,
Saying, 'Give to me my ain [own] wee son,
And take thee of thy nourris [nurse's] fee.
And it shall come to pass on a summer's day,
When the Sun shines bright on every stone,

I'll come and fetch my ain wee son,

And teach him how to swim the foam.

And ye shall marry a gunner good,

And a gey [very] good gunner I'm sure he'll be,

And the very first shot that e'er he shoots

Will kill both my young son and me.'

Note: Sule Skerry is a rock off the coast of Hoy in the Orkney Islands.

As is typical of folk ballads, the story begins abruptly, moves rapidly, and is told as an impersonal narrative, primarily through dialogue and action. Also, as is typical, the ballad deals with a single episode, with minimal imagery or background information, and little attempt to develop character.

Traditional attributes of the shaman include both the ability to shape-shift and the power of divination, and the silkie in this ballad is master of both.

Divination is defined in the Introduction to Loewe and Blacker's *Divination and Oracles* (1981) as "the attempt to elicit from some higher power or supernatural being the answers to questions beyond the range of ordinary human understanding". And if we concur with the belief that such techniques enable us to catalyze our own unconscious knowledge (see Von Franz, 1980, p.38), then divination can also be claimed to be the attempt to elicit the answers to such questions from what is commonly referred to in New Age texts as the "inner shaman".

History indicates that divination has always been popular, probably because it caters for a basic and universal human desire to be able to remove uncertainty and to predict the future. Its practice can be traced back into the distant past and by Biblical times it was clearly widespread.

Although many people consider divination to be a practice that goes against the grain of traditional Christian beliefs, in both the Old and New Testament we find holy men practising the casting of lots. It is related (Joshua 7:14 sqq.) that Joshua, at the Lord's command, pronounced sentence by lot on Achan who had stolen of the anathema. Again Saul, by drawing lots, found that his son Jonathan had eaten honey (1 Kings 14:58 sqq.). Zacharias was chosen by lot to offer incense (Luke 1:9) and the apostles by drawing lots elected Matthias to the apostleship (Acts 1:26). Therefore it would seem that divination by lots was not unlawful, at least not when practised by those who were considered to have the right to do so.

Of course we also know that in Biblical times the casting of lots was commonly practised in the Middle East by peoples outside the Judaic and Christian traditions. Take the case of the mariners who transport Jonah from Joppa to Tarshish, for example, who cast lots to ascertain the cause of the evil that befalls them (Jonah 1:7).

One of the problems we are faced with when it comes to a study of divination is that despite millennia of "field testing," divination has no scientific validation. "Due to lack of controlled observations–the result of academic indifference, it is extremely difficult to refer to well organized field work on the functional outcome of divination practices. Anecdotal reports are more common but have only limited scientific value" (Frecska & Luna, 2007, p.138).

Diverging, unsystematic explanations are put forward by academics to account for the recorded successes of divination practices. On the other hand, indigenous healers of different cultures are unequivocal in their interpretation of how divination takes place, firmly and unquestionably believing it to be through the guidance of the spirits (see Frecska & Luna, 2007, p.139), and for the "insider", this is explanation enough. In any case, as "It is untenable to make statements from one form of consciousness regarding the reality of the other" (Frecska & Luna, 2007, p.143), in one sense it is a question that can never be answered to the satisfaction of all parties involved. The scientific explanation will fail to satisfy the insider, and the explanation offered by the insider will fail to satisfy the scientist.

However, if it is accepted that "the whole Universe is an interconnected, entangled totality ... [then it has to be assumed that] consciousness is inherently nonlocal as well" (Frecska & Luna, 2007, p.148). In ASCs (altered states of consciousness) this, by all accounts, is what becomes apparent, which is why indigenous shamans induce such states for various purposes, including that of divination–to serve their communities. Neo-shamanic practitioners enter ASCs too, but not always to serve the community like the indigenous shaman. This is because they do not necessarily form part of such a clearly defined community. Consequently, there may well be times when they serve the individual rather than the group.

Describing one's own experience of sacred reality in terms that are both understandable and acceptable can prove to be quite a problem for those of us involved in shamanic practice. How, for example, can you convince an observer that you travelled to the Upper World and met your Sacred Teacher when all he saw was you lying on the floor with your eyes closed as if you were sleeping? Indeed, offering any kind of explanation is often more trouble than it is worth, which might well be why those of us who are actively involved in Neo-shamanism tend not to talk about what we practise unless pressed to do so. The fact of the matter is that

'Without direct experience, talk of ASC experiences can [only] remain at the level of what the philosopher Immanuel Kant famously called "empty concepts," concepts devoid of the richness, meaning, and significance that only direct experience can impart. [And] This deficit can be dangerously distorting' (Walsh, 2007, p.90).

Perhaps this is why, instead of attempting to talk about such experiences, the preference has been to write shamanic stories and / or shamanic ballads through which they can be presented in a more palatable form, as far as the outsider is concerned.

Encounter-narratives presented by cunning folk and witches, and recorded in early modern European witch trials, provide evidence to suggest that "popular shamanistic visionary traditions, of pre-Christian origin, survived in many parts of Britain during the early modern period" (Wilby, 2005, p.7). And these traditions can be found reflected in both our folk-tales and our ballads.

"Although healing, finding lost goods and identifying criminals were central concerns for a large proportion of cunning folk, they also ...possessed a range of other skills. Many were believed capable of divining the future and it was not uncommon for them to be asked to make predictions [as the man-silkie does in this ballad], and give subsequent advice, on a wide variety of matters" (Wilby, 2005, p.39). They were also valued for their role as mediators between the living and the dead. And, like witches, cunning folk claimed to perform magic with the help of familiar spirits, who can be regarded as the equivalent of the spirit helpers that shamans work with. According to information collected in trial records, the initial meetings between cunning folk and their familiars would often be spontaneous, sudden and unexpected, though sometimes the familiar would be received as a gift from another magical practitioner. These familiars were used by cunning folk in various ways - in healing, to help discover the whereabouts of lost goods, to identify criminals, to divine the future, and / or to converse with the dead. And the long-term and usually intimate working relationships established were characterized by journeys to other worlds, such as fairyland, where it was possible for the journeyer to "enjoy feasting, drinking, dancing, music, flight experiences, animal metamorphosis and the learning and performing of magic" (Wilby, 2005, pp.92-93).

It has been suggested that even though they are given different cultural expression at particular times and places, the traits which underpin Siberian shamanism occur naturally in individuals throughout humanity (see Hutton, 2001, p.149). "The uncanny similarity between the encounter-experience of the early modern cunning folk and witches and those of nineteenth- and early twentieth-century Siberian and Native American shamans are therefore wholly in keeping with the trans-historical and trans-cultural congruity of shamanistic experience" (Wilby, 2005, pp.183-184).

Although it cannot be proved conclusively, given all the parallels between the experiences of cunning folk and witches and those of tribal shamans, it is highly likely that shamanism was once widely practised in pre-Christian Europe, and that we should have shamanic ballads that reflect this should therefore come as no surprise.

What we have is "An oral legacy ... as old as mankind and woven out of infinitesimal threads. A complex inheritance of magical beliefs and practices worked together over a millennia to form vivid and charismatic mythological and cosmological tapestries" (Wilby, 2005, pp.254-255). And it is a legacy to treasure and cherish.

The Silkie is of course not the only shape-shifter to be found in

The Asrai

the sea. There is also the ubiquitous mermaid as well as the less familiar merman.

The Fisherman and the Merman

OF mermen and merwomen many strange stories are told in the Shetland Isles. Beneath the depths of the ocean, according to these stories, an atmosphere exists adapted to the respiratory organs of certain beings, resembling in form the human race, possessed of surpassing beauty, of limited supernatural powers, and liable to the incident of death. They dwell in a wide territory of the globe, far below the region of fishes, over which the sea, like the cloudy canopy of our sky, loftily rolls, and they possess habitations constructed of the pearl and coral productions of the ocean. Having lungs not adapted to a watery medium, but to the nature of atmospheric air, it would be impossible for them to pass through the volume of waters that intervenes between the submarine and supramarine world, if it were not for the extraordinary power they inherit of entering the skin of some animal capable of existing in the sea, which they are enabled to occupy by a sort of demoniacal possession. One shape they put on is that of an animal human above the waist, yet terminating below in the tail and fins of a fish, but the most favourite form is that of the larger seal or Haaf-fish; for, in possessing an amphibious nature, they are enabled not only to exist in the ocean, but to land on some rock, where they frequently lighten themselves of their sea-dress, resume their proper shape, and with much curiosity examine the nature of the upper world belonging to the human race. Unfortunately, however, each merman or merwoman possesses but one skin, enabling the individual to ascend the seas, and if, on visiting the abode of man, the garb be lost, the hapless being must unavoidably become an inhabitant of the earth.

A story is told of a boat's crew who landed for the purpose of attacking the seals lying in the hollows of the crags at one of the stacks. The men stunned a number of the animals, and while they were in this state stripped them of their skins, with the fat attached to them. Leaving the carcases on the rock, the crew were about to set off for the shore of Papa Stour, when such a tremendous swell arose that every one flew quickly to the boat. All succeeded in entering it except one man, who had imprudently lingered behind. The crew were unwilling to leave a companion to perish on the skerries, but the surge increased so fast that after many unsuccessful attempts to bring the boat close in to the stack the unfortunate wight was left to his fate. A stormy night came on, and the deserted Shetlander saw no prospect before him but that of perishing from cold and hunger, or of being washed into the sea by the breakers which threatened to dash over the rocks. At length he perceived many of the seals, who in their flight had escaped the attack of the boatmen, approach the skerry [rocks which are submerged at high tide], disrobe themselves of their amphibious hides, and resume the shape of the sons and daughters of the ocean. Their first object was to assist in the recovery of their friends, who, having been stunned by clubs, had, while in that state, been deprived of their skins. When the flayed animals had regained their sensibility, they assumed their proper form of mermen or merwomen, and began to lament in a mournful lay, wildly accompanied by the storm that was raging around, the loss of their sea-dress, which would prevent them from again enjoying their native azure atmosphere and coral mansions that lay below the deep waters of the Atlantic. But their chief lamentation was for Ollavitinus, the son of Gioga, who, having been stripped of his seal's skin, would be forever parted from his mates, and condemned to become an outcast inhabitant of the upper world. Their song was at length broken off by observing one of their enemies viewing, with shivering limbs and looks of comfortless despair, the wild waves that dashed over the stack. Gioga immediately conceived the idea of rendering subservient to the advantage of her son the perilous situation of the man. She addressed him with mildness, proposing to carry him safe on her back across the sea to Papa Stour, on condition of receiving the seal's skin of Ollavitinus. A bargain was struck, and Gioga clad herself in her amphibious garb; but the Shetlander, alarmed at the sight of the stormy main that he was to ride through, prudently begged leave of the matron, for his better preservation, that he might be allowed to cut a few holes in her shoulders and flanks, in order to procure, between the skin and the flesh, a better, fastening for his hands and feet. The request being complied with, the man grasped the neck of the seal, and committing himself to her care, she landed him safely at Acres Gio in Papa Stour; from which place he immediately repaired to a skeo [a hut for drying fish in] at Hamna Voe, where the skin was deposited, and honourably fulfilled his part of the contract by affording Gioga the means whereby her son could again revisit the ethereal space over which the sea spread its green mantle.

Taken from *Scottish Fairy and Folk-tales* Selected and Edited with an Introduction by Sir George Douglas A. L. Burt Company, New York [1901?]. Scanned, proofed and formatted at sacred-texts.com April, 2003, by J. B. Hare. This text is in the public domain in the US because it was published prior to 1923.

We have so far encountered the silkie, mermaids and mermen,

and now we come to perhaps the least well-known water spirit of them all:

The Asrai

One Moonlit night, a man was out fishing on one of Cheshire's deep meres when he felt something unusually heavy in his net. Hauling it on board, he was amazed to find in its meshes a beautiful, naked girl with long, green hair, webbed fingers and toes, and no larger than a twelve-year-old child.

Recovering from his initial shock, he recalled having heard tales of the Asrai, a race of shy, gentle water spirits which inhabited the deepest lakes; who only grew by the light of the full Moon, and who only surfaced once a century. He had always discounted such stories as myth, but now the evidence lay before him, tangled in his net, struggling to get free. Indeed it, or she, appeared to be trying to tell him something, and was pointing in some agitation to the Moon, which was by now setting. But her speech, which was soft, like ripples in the water, was incomprehensible to him.

Her evident distress caused him some discomfort and the fisherman had half-a-mind to set it free. On the other hand, he wanted to show it to his children, and then he began to think how the rich folk in the castle might like to show it in their fish-ponds, and would pay him well. So he hardened his heart, and instead began the long row homewards.

The Asrai managed to get one arm out of the net, and pointed again and again to the waning Moon, and then laid a hand on his arm, – 'like cool foam, the touch was,' he said later. But it seemed that his human warmth hurt it, for then it shrank away from him, and curled up in the bottom of the boat, covering herself with her long, green hair.

Remembering how the Asrai were said to be afraid of daylight, he then placed some rushes over her, and rowed long and hard for the lake shore, simply, turning a deaf ear to the creature's faint cries. It was not until Sunrise that he arrived back at his jetty, where he was eager to uncover his find.

However pulling back the rushes revealed nothing but a pool of water; the Asrai had vanished, and he was left with nothing but the mark on his arm to show for his efforts, a mark that never went away.

Compiled and adapted from various versions of the story in Ruth Tongue, *Forgotten Folk-Tales of the English Counties*, Routledge and Kegan Paul, (1970).

The Asrai were believed to be a race of water-fairies who brought good fortune to the country round about. They were gentle and good and very shy and no one ever saw them. They lived in deep waters and were like beautiful men and women but their hair was green like floating water-weeds and their hands and feet were webbed. Once every hundred years at night they would come to the surface to look at the Moon and grow and that would be when someone saw one, so that folk still remembered they really were there. They said, too, that if an Asrai looked on the light of day it died.

This story reverses the more usual state of affairs, where men are the victims of female water spirits, who use their beauty to lure infatuated men to their deaths. In this case however it is the Asrai's beauty that results in her death, as the fisherman cannot bear to let her go.

The main interest in this rare legend lies in the very clear description of these gentle, shy water people. They seem akin to the Welsh morgans (lake spirits) in their love of deep water, and to the Highland fuath (a malicious and dangerous fairy) in their inability to live in daylight.

As for the 'paralysed limb' motif, it comes up occasionally in stories where a person touches a supernatural creature, or is touched by one, though the effects are usually more severe than those described in the tale of the Asrai.

Bibliography

Berman, M. (2008) *Divination and the Shamanic Story*, Newcastle: Cambridge Scholars Publishing.

Buchan, David. 'Talerole Analysis and Child's Supernatural Ballads.' In Harris, J. (ed.) (1991) *The Ballad and Oral Literature*, Cambridge, Massachusetts: Harvard University Press.

Child, F. J. *Scottish and English Popular Ballads*, http://www.sacred-texts.com/neu/eng/child/ch113.htm

Eliade, M. (1989) *Shamanism: Archaic techniques of ecstasy*, London: Arkana (published in the USA by Pantheon Books 1964).

Eliade, M. (1991) *Images and Symbols*, New Jersey: Princeton University Press (The original edition is copyright Librairie Gallimard 1952).

Frecska, E. & Luna, L.E. (2007) 'The Shamanic Healer: Master of Nonlocal Information.' In Shaman Vol. 15 Nos. 1 & 2.

Loewe, M., & Blacker, C. (eds.) (1981) *Divination and Oracles*, London: George Allen & Unwin Ltd.

Orkneyjar - a website dedicated to the preserving, exploring and documenting the ancient history, folklore and traditions of Orkney - a group of islands lying off the northern tip of Scotland, where the North Sea and the Atlantic Ocean meet. http://www.orkneyjar.com/folklore/selkiefolk/

Harner, M. (1990 3rd Edition) *The Way of the Shaman*, Harper & Row (first published by Harper & Row in 1980).

Hutton, R. (2001) *Shamans: Siberian Spirituality and the Western Imagination*, London: Hambeldon & London.

Shaw, S. & Francis, A. (eds.) (2008) *Deep Blue: Critical reflections on Nature, Religion and Water*, London: Equinox Publishing Ltd.

Scandinavian Centre for Shamanic Studies http://www.shaman-center.dk

Von Franz, M.L. (1980) *On Divination and Synchronicity*, Toronto, Canada: Inner City Books.

Walsh, R.N. (2007) *The World of Shamanism: New Views of an Ancient Tradition*, Woodbury, Minnesota: Llewellyn Publications.

Wilby, E. (2005) *Cunning Folk and Familiar Spirits: Shamanistic Visionary Traditions in Early Modern British Witchcraft and Magic*, Brighton: Sussex Academic Press.

Merman-Flying-Fish

The Prince Who Thought He Was a Turkey: NLP Revisited

We are all familiar with fairy tales about frogs turning into princes, but probably not about princes turning into turkeys – which is what the next story is all about.

NLP stands for Neuro-Linguistic Programming. It has been described as the practical psychology of how to use the mind to consistently achieve goals in all areas of life. Neuro refers to the nervous system by which our experiences are processed via the five senses. Linguistic refers to language and also non-verbal communication systems through which our experiences are coded, ordered and given meaning. Programming refers to the ability to discover, utilize and change the patterns that we run in our thinking, feeling and behaving. Your thinking and feeling shape your experience of the world. Changing the patterns of your thinking and feeling changes your reality, and the aim of NLP is to change it for the better.

NLP was first developed at the University of California, Santa Cruz in the period of 1973-1979, where John Grinder, Richard Bandler, and Gregory Bateson were all based.

Rapport is the foundation for any meaningful interaction between two or more people – rapport is about establishing an environment of trust and understanding, to respect and honour the other person's world, which gives a person the freedom to fully express their ideas and concerns and to know they will be respected by the other person(s).

Most of our communication, as much as 93%, transpires nonverbally and unconsciously. NLP rapport skills teach us how to communicate at that unconscious level. The key to establishing rapport is an ability to enter another person's world by assuming a similar state of mind. The first thing to do is to become more like the other person by matching and mirroring the person's behaviours. Matching and mirroring is a powerful way of getting an appreciation of how the other person is seeing/experiencing the world. If your partner is using many visual words, you should also use mainly visual words and similarly for auditory, kinaesthetic and auditory digital words.

There is, however, nothing new about this knowledge, as the following story, written more than two hundred years ago, clearly illustrates. This story, by Rabbi Nachman of Bratislav, the great grandson of the Baal Shem Tov, was adapted from Shulman, Y.D. (1993) *The Chambers of the Palace: Teachings of Rabbi Nachman of Bratislav*, Northvale, New Jersey: Jason Aronson Inc.

The Prince Who Thought
He Was a Turkey

Once there was a prince who thought he was a turkey. He sat naked underneath a table and pecked at bones and pieces of bread. All the doctors despaired of healing him, and the king was very sad.

Then a wise man came and said, "Don't worry. I've got the answer to the problem. Just watch and do what I tell you."

The wise man took off his clothes and sat under the table next to the prince, and he also pecked at crumbs and bones.

The prince asked him, "Who are you? What are you doing here?"

The wise man answered, "And what are you doing here?"

"I'm a rooster."

"I'm also a rooster."

The two of them sat there for some time until they got used to each other. Then the wise man gave a signal, and a shirt was thrown down.

The wise man said to the prince, "Do you think that a rooster can't wear a shirt? One can wear a shirt and still be a rooster." So both of them put on shirts.

After a while, he signalled again, and a pair of trousers was thrown down to him. He said, "Do you think if someone wears pants, he can't be a rooster?" This went on until they were both dressed.

Afterwards, he signalled, and human food was thrown down from the table. He said to the prince, "Do you think if you eat good food, you're no longer a turkey? One can eat and still be a turkey." So they both ate.

After that, he told the prince. "Do you think that a turkey can only sit under the table? One can sit at the table and still be a turkey."

And he continued to act in this way until he completely cured the prince.

If you plan to use the story in class, then here is a possible follow-up activity that could actually be used with any story you ever tell a group of students.

Choose a couple of the following questions to ask the person sitting next to you. Then report back what you found out to the rest of the class:

a. What feelings did you have during the telling of the story?

b. Have you ever been in a similar situation to any of the characters in the tale?

c. Did any of the characters remind you of people you know?

d. What do you think the "message" of the story is?

e. Did it remind you of any other stories you know?

f. Which was the most moving or memorable bit of the story for you?

g. Which bit of the story sent you off to sleep?

Here are some further ideas for follow-up work that could be used for a teacher development workshop:

a. If you were reborn as an animal, which animal would you like, or, wouldn't you like, to be and why?

b. Have you ever known, or been taught by, a teacher you thought shouldn't have been one or who acted as if he/she was something else?

c. Working in small groups, choose one of the following titles and write the story to accompany it:

The Teacher Who Thought He/She Knew All the Answers

The Teacher Who Thought He/She Was Unworthy

The Teacher Who Longed To Be Someone Else

(Ideally, the story should involve an intervention that brings about a change for the better to the poor miserable soul's condition).

The Frog's Skin

The transformed husband, wife or lover is a common theme in fairy tales. "Beauty and the Beast," from 18th-century France, is probably the best known "animal bridegroom" story, but there are many others. In "East of the Sun, West of the Moon", from Scandinavia, the heroine is actually married to the Beast (who is, in this case, a big white bear) at the beginning of the story, before he regains his human shape. Each night he comes to the marriage bed changed back into his human form. His wife is forbidden to see his face, but of course she soon breaks this taboo and must complete a series of arduous tasks before she wins him back again. In "Brother and Sister" from Germany, two siblings run away from their wicked stepmother through a dark, fearsome, enchanted wood. The path of escape lies across three streams, and at each crossing the brother stops to drink. Each time the sister begs him not to, but at the third stream he cannot resist. He bends down to the water in the shape of a man, and rises again in the shape of a stag. From then on, the sister and her brother-stag live alone at the heart of the forest. A king comes to hunt the magnificent stag — but it is the sister he claims and carries from the wood. Eventually, with his sister's help, the boy resumes his true shape. In "The White Deer," found in Germany, Scandinavia, France and the Scottish highlands, a wellborn girl is cursed in her crib by a slighted fairy. She must not see the Sun before her wedding day or disaster will strike. On her way to be wed, the sun penetrates her carriage; she turns into a deer and disappears through the wildwood. She is hunted and wounded by her own fiancé as she roams sadly through the forest.

The fairy tale in which a frog is kissed by a princess and then turns into a handsome young prince is also for many of us a familiar one. However, in the tale included here, from the Republic of Georgia, the gender roles are reversed. Before presenting the story though, some background notes on the land it comes from.

Georgians call themselves Kartvelebi and their land Sakartvelo, names derived from a Pagan god called Kartlos, said to be the father of all Georgians. As for how they came to possess the land they consider to be the most beautiful in the world, legend has it that when God was distributing portions of the world to all the peoples of the Earth, the Georgians were having a party and doing some serious drinking at the time. As a result they arrived later than everyone else and were told by God that all the land had already been distributed. When they replied that they were late only because they had been raising their glasses in praise of Him, God was pleased and gave the Georgians that part of Earth he had been saving for himself.

Holding on to their land has never been easy though, and invasions have been frequent. The Arabs conquered Tbilisi (Tiflis) in the 7th century, and the Turks began their forays into Georgia in the 11th century. The Mongol hordes led by Tamerlane devastated eastern Georgia no less than eight times in the 1380s and 1390s. For most of the period since then Georgia has been under foreign rule, for many centuries divided between the Persian and Ottoman empires. In 1784, in a desperate move to secure protection from the Turks and Persians, King Irakli II placed his kingdom under the sovereignty of the Russian throne, and so it remained until recently, save for a brief period of autonomy after the Soviet Revolution. In April 1991 though, the Republic of Georgia declared its independence from the USSR.

While the more accessible central lowlands have served as a virtual crossroads between Orient and Occident, the inhabitants of the northern Georgian mountain districts, both east and west of the Likhi range, have held on to their ancient folkways and pre-Christian religious systems to a degree unparalleled in modern Europe. Until very recently, oracles (kadagebi) practised their trade within a few dozen kilometers of Tbilisi; animal sacrifices and the pouring of libations, traditions reminiscent of Homeric Greece, are still commonly observed in many parts of the country.

And now the time has come for the story:

The Transformed Wife

THERE were once three brothers who wished to marry. They said: 'Let us each shoot an arrow, and each shall take his wife from the place where the arrow falls.' They shot their arrows; those of the two elder brothers fell on noblemen's houses, while the youngest brother's arrow fell in a lake. The two elder brothers led home their noble wives, and the youngest went to the shore of the lake. He saw a frog creep out of the lake and sit down upon a stone. He took it up and carried it back to the house. All the brothers came home with what fate had given them; the elder brothers with the noble maidens, and the youngest with a frog.

The brothers went out to work, the wives prepared the dinner, and attended to all their household duties; the frog sat by the fire croaking, and its eyes glittered. Thus they lived together a long time in love and harmony.

At last the sisters-in-law wearied of the sight of the frog; when they swept the house, they threw out the frog with the dust. If the youngest brother found it, he took it up in his hand; if not, the frog would leap back to its place by the fire and begin to croak. The noble sisters did not like this, and said to their husbands: 'Drive this frog out, and get a real wife for your brother.' Every day the brothers bothered the youngest. He replied, saying: 'This frog is certainly my fate, I am worthy of no better, I must be faithful to it.' His sisters-in-law persisted in telling their husbands that the brother and his frog must be sent away, and at last they agreed.

The young brother was now left quite desolate: there was no one to make his food, no one to stand watching at the door. For a short time a neighbouring woman came to wait upon him, but she had no time, so he was left alone. The man became very melancholy.

Once when he was thinking sadly of his loneliness, he went to work. When he had finished his day's labour, he went home. He looked into his house and was struck with amazement. The sideboard was well replenished; in one place was spread a cloth, and on the cloth were many different kinds of tempting viands. He looked and saw the frog in its place croaking. He said to himself that his sisters-in-law must have done this for him, and went to his work again. He was out all day working, and when he came home he always found everything prepared for him.

Once he said to himself: 'I will see for once who is this unseen benefactor, who comes to do good to me and look after me.' That day he stayed at home; he seated himself on the roof of the house and watched. In a short time the frog leaped out of the fireplace, jumped over to the doors, and all round the room; seeing no one there, it went back and took off the frog's skin, put it near the fire, and came forth a beautiful maiden, fair as the Sun; so lovely was she that man could not imagine anything prettier. In the twinkling of an eye she had tidied everything, prepared the food and cooked it. When everything was ready, she went to the fire, put on the skin again, and began to croak. When the man saw this he was very much astonished; he rejoiced exceedingly that God had granted him such happiness. He descended from the roof, went in, caressed his frog tenderly, and then sat down to his tasty supper.

The next day the man hid himself in the place where he had been the day before. The frog, having satisfied itself that nobody was there, stripped off its skin and began its good work. This time the man stole silently into the house, seized the frog's skin in his hand and threw it into the fire. When the maiden saw this she entreated him, she wept—she said: 'Do not burn it, or thou shalt surely be destroyed' —but the man had burnt it in a moment. 'Now, if thy happiness be turned to misery, it is not my fault,' said the sorrow-stricken woman.

In a very short time the whole country-side knew that the man who had a frog now possessed in its place a lovely woman, who had come to him from heaven.

The lord of the country heard of this, and wished to take her from him. He called the beautiful woman's husband to him and said: 'Sow a barnful of wheat in a day, or give me thy wife.' When he had spoken thus, the man was obliged to consent, and he went home melancholy.

When he went in he told his wife what had taken place. She reproached him, saying: 'I told thee what would happen if thou didst burn the skin, and thou didst not heed me; but I will not blame thee. Be not sad; go in the morning to the edge of the lake from which I came, and call out: "Mother and Father! I pray you, lend me your swift bullocks"—lead them away with thee, and the bullocks will in one day plough the fields and sow the grain.' The husband did this.

He went to the edge of the lake and called out: 'Mother and Father! I entreat you, lend me your swift bullocks today.' There came forth from the lake such a team of oxen as was never seen on sea or land.

The youth drove the bullocks away, came to his lord's fields, and ploughed and sowed them in one day.

His lord was very much surprised. He did not know if there was anything impossible to this man, whose wife he wanted. He called him a second time, and said: 'Go and gather up the wheat thou hast sown, that not a grain may be wanting, and that the barn may be full. If thou dost not this, thy wife is mine.'

'This is impossible,' said the man to himself. He went home to his wife, who again reproached him, and then said: 'Go to the lake's edge and ask for the jackdaws.'

The husband went to the edge of the lake and called out: 'Mother and Father! I beg you to lend me your jackdaws to-day.' From the lake came forth flocks of jackdaws; they flew to the ploughed ground, each gathered up a seed and put it into the barn.

The lord came and cried out: 'There is one seed short; I know each one, and one is missing.' At that moment a jackdaw's caw was heard; it came with the missing seed, but owing to a lame foot it was a little late.

The lord was very angry that even the impossible was possible to this man, and could not think what to give him to do.

He puzzled his brain until he thought of the following plan. He called the man and said to him: 'My mother, who died in this village, took with her a ring. If thou goest to the other world and bringest that ring hither to me, it is well; if not, I shall take away thy wife.'

The man said to himself: 'This is quite impossible.' He went home and complained to his wife. She reproached him, and then said: 'Go to the lake and ask for the ram.' The husband went to the lake and called out: 'Mother and Father! give me your ram to-day, I pray you.' From the lake there came forth a ram with twisted horns; from its mouth issued a flame of fire. It said to the man: 'Mount on my back!'

The man sat down, and, quick as lightning, the ram descended towards the lower regions. It went on and shot like an arrow through the Earth.

They travelled on, and saw in one place a man and woman sitting on a bullock's skin, which was not big enough for them, and they were like to fall off. The man called out to them: 'What can be the meaning of this, that this bullock skin is not big enough for two people?' They said: 'We have seen many pass by like thee, but none has returned. When thou comest back we shall answer thy question.'

They went on their way and saw a man and woman sitting on an axe-handle, and they were not afraid of falling. The man called out to them: 'Are you not afraid of falling from the handle of an axe?' They said to him: 'We have seen many pass by like thee, but none has returned. When thou comest back we shall answer thy question.'

They went on their way again, until they came to a place where they saw a priest feeding cattle. This priest had such a long beard that it spread over the ground, and the cattle, instead of eating grass, fed on the priest's beard, and he could not prevent it. The man called out: 'Priest, what is the meaning of this? why is thy beard pasture for these cattle?' The priest replied: 'I have seen many pass by like thee, but none has returned. When thou comest back I shall answer thy question.'

They journeyed on again until they came to a place where they saw nothing but boiling pitch, and a flame came forth from it—and this was hell. The ram said: 'Sit firmly on my back, for we must pass through this fire.' The man held fast, the ram gave a leap, and they escaped through the fire unhurt.

There they saw a melancholy woman seated on a golden throne. She said: 'What is it, my child? What troubles thee? What has brought thee here?' He told her everything that had happened to him. She said: 'I must punish this very wicked child of mine, and thou must take him a casket from me.' She gave him a casket, and said: 'Whatever thou dost, do not open this casket thyself, take it with thee, give it to thy lord, and run quickly away from him.'

The man took the casket and went away. He came to the place where the priest was feeding the cattle. The priest said: 'I promised thee an answer; hearken unto my words. In life I loved nothing but myself, I cared for nought else. My flocks I fed on other pastures than my own, and the neighbouring cattle died of starvation; now I am paying the penalty.'

Then he went on to the place where the man and woman were sitting on the handle of the axe. They said: 'We promised thee an answer; hearken unto our words. We loved each other too well on Earth, and it is the same with us here.'

Then he came to the two seated on the bullock skin, which was not big enough for them. They said: 'We promised thee an answer; hearken unto our words. We despised each other in life, and we equally despise each other here.'

At last the man came up on Earth, descended from the ram, and went to his lord. He gave him the casket and quickly ran away. The lord opened the casket, and there came forth fire, which swallowed him up. Our brother was thus victorious over his enemy, and no one took his wife from him. They lived lovingly together, and blessed God as their deliverer.

Taken from *Georgian Folk-Tales*, by Marjory Wardrop. Originally published by David Nutt in the Strand, London [1894] Scanned, proofed and formatted at sacred-texts.com, July 2006, by John Bruno Hare. This text is in the public domain in the United States because it was published prior to 1923.

The Ugly Duckling and Making a Death Doll

 ❝The Ugly Duckling" (Danish: Den grimme ælling) is a literary fairy tale by Danish poet and author Hans Christian Andersen. The story tells of a homely little bird born in a barnyard who suffers much verbal and physical abuse from the other birds and animals on the farm until, much to his delight (and to the surprise of others), he matures into a beautiful swan, the most beautiful bird of all. The tale, beloved around the world as a tale about personal transformation for the better, is completely Andersen's invention and owes no debt to fairy or folklore. It was first published in Copenhagen, Denmark, 11 November 1843 in *New Fairy Tales. First Book. First Collection.*

Andersen first conceived the story in 1842 while enjoying the beauty of nature during his stay at the country estate of Bregentved, and lavished a year's worth of attention upon it. He initially considered "The Young Swans" as the tale's title but, not wanting to spoil the element of surprise in the protagonist's transformation, discarded it for "The Ugly Duckling". He later confessed that the story was "a reflection of my own life", and, when the critic Georg Brandes questioned Andersen about whether he would write his autobiography, the poet claimed that it had already been written — "The Ugly Duckling".

The suggestion that the tale is to a certain extent auto-biographical is reinforced by what we know about the personal details of the writer's life. In reviewing *Hans Christian Andersen: A New Life* by biographer Jens Andersen, British journalist Anne Chisholm writes

"Andersen himself was a tall, ugly boy with a big nose and big feet, and when he grew up with a beautiful singing voice and a passion for the theatre he was cruelly teased and mocked by other children". It is also likely that Andersen was the illegitimate son of Prince Christian Frederik (later King Christian VIII of Denmark), and that he found this out some time before he wrote the tale.

The Ugly Duckling

It was summer in the land of Denmark, and though for most of the year the country looks flat and ugly, it was beautiful now. The wheat was yellow, the oats were green, the hay was dry and delicious to roll in, and from the old ruined house which nobody lived in, down to the edge of the canal, was a forest of great burdocks, so tall that a whole family of children might have dwelt in them and never have been found out.

It was under these burdocks that a duck had built herself a warm nest, and was not sitting all day on six pretty eggs. Five of them were white, but the sixth, which was larger than the others, was of an ugly grey colour. The duck was always puzzled about that egg, and how it came to be so different from the rest. Other birds might have thought that when the duck went down in the morning and evening to the water to stretch her legs in a good swim, some lazy mother might have been on the watch, and have popped her egg into the nest. But ducks are not clever at all, and are not quick at counting, so this duck did not worry herself about the matter, but just took care that the big egg should be as warm as the rest.

This was the first set of eggs that the duck had ever laid, and, to begin with, she was very pleased and proud, and laughed at the other mothers, who were always neglecting their duties to gossip with each other or to take little extra swims besides the two in the morning and evening that were necessary for health. But at length she grew tired of sitting there all day. 'Surely eggs take longer hatching than they did,' she said to herself; and she pined for a little amusement also. Still, she knew that if she left her eggs and the ducklings in them to die none of her friends would ever speak to her again; so there she stayed, only getting off the eggs several times a day to see if the shells were cracking—which may have been the very reason why they did not crack sooner.

She had looked at the eggs at least a hundred and fifty times, when, to her joy, she saw a tiny crack on two of them, and scrambling back to the nest she drew the eggs closer the one to the other, and never moved for the whole of that day. Next morning she was rewarded by noticing cracks in the whole five eggs, and by midday two little yellow heads were poking out from the shells. This encouraged her so much that, after breaking the shells with her bill, so that the little creatures could get free of them, she sat steadily for a whole night upon the nest, and before the Sun arose the five white eggs were empty, and ten pairs of eyes were gazing out upon the green world.

Now the duck had been carefully brought up, and did not like dirt, and, besides, broken shells are not at all comfortable things to sit or walk upon; so she pushed the rest out over the side, and felt delighted to have some company to talk to till the big egg hatched. But day after day went on, and the big egg showed no signs of cracking, and the duck grew more and more impatient, and began to wish to consult her husband, who never came.

'I can't think what is the matter with it,' the duck grumbled to her neighbour who had called in to pay her a visit. 'Why I could have hatched two broods in the time that this one has taken!'

'Let me look at it,' said the old neighbour. 'Ah, I thought so; it is a turkey's egg. Once, when I was young, they tricked me to sitting on a brood of turkey's eggs myself, and when they were hatched the creatures were so stupid that nothing would make them learn to swim. I have no patience when I think of it.'

'Well, I will give it another chance,' sighed the duck, 'and if it does not come out of its shell in another twenty-four hours, I will just leave it alone and teach the rest of them to swim properly and to find their own food. I really can't be expected to do two things at once.' And with a fluff of her feathers she pushed the egg into the middle of the nest.

All through the next day she sat on, giving up even her morning bath for fear that a blast of cold might strike the big egg. In the evening, when she ventured to peep, she thought she saw a tiny crack in the upper part of the shell. Filled with hope, she went back to her duties, though she could hardly sleep all night for excitement. When she woke with the first streaks of light she felt something stirring under her. Yes, there it was at last; and as she moved, a big awkward bird tumbled head foremost on the ground.

There was no denying it was ugly, even the mother was forced to admit that to herself, though she only said it was 'large' and 'strong.' 'You won't need any teaching when you are once in the water,' she told him, with a glance of surprise at the dull brown which covered his back, and at his long naked neck. And indeed he did not, though he was not half so pretty to look at as the little yellow balls that followed her.

When they returned they found the old neighbour on the bank waiting for them to take them into the duckyard. 'No, it is not a young turkey, certainly,' whispered she in confidence to the mother, 'for though it is lean and skinny, and has no colour to speak of, yet there is something rather distinguished about it, and it holds its head up well.'

'It is very kind of you to say so,' answered the mother, who by this time had some secret doubts of its loveliness. 'Of course, when you see it by itself it is all right, though it is different, somehow, from the others. But one cannot expect all one's children to be beautiful!'

By this time they had reached the centre of the yard, where a very old duck was sitting, who was treated with great respect by all the fowls present.

'You must go up and bow low before her,' whispered the mother to her children, nodding her head in the direction of the old lady, 'and keep your legs well apart, as you see me do. No well-bred duckling turns in its toes. It is a sign of common parents.'

The little ducks tried hard to make their small fat bodies copy the movements of their mother, and the old lady was quite pleased with them; but the rest of the ducks looked on discontentedly, and said to each other:

'Oh, dear me, here are ever so many more! The yard is full already; and did you ever see anything quite as ugly as that great tall creature? He is a disgrace to any brood. I shall go and chase him out!' So saying she put up her feathers, and running to the big duckling bit his neck.

The duckling gave a loud quack; it was the first time he had felt any pain, and at the sound his mother turned quickly. 'Leave him alone,' she said fiercely, 'or I will send for his father. He was not troubling you.'

'No; but he is so ugly and awkward no one can put up with him,' answered the stranger. And though the duckling did not understand the meaning of the words, he felt he was being blamed, and became more uncomfortable still when the old Spanish duck who ruled the fowlyard struck in:

'It certainly is a great pity he is so different from these beautiful darlings. If he could only be hatched over again!'

The poor little fellow drooped his head, and did not know where to look, but was comforted when his mother answered:

'He may not be quite as handsome as the others, but he swims better, and is very strong; I am sure he will make his way in the world as well as anybody.'

'Well, you must feel quite at home here,' said the old duck waddling off. And so they did, all except the duckling, who was snapped at by everyone when they thought his mother was not looking. Even the turkey-cock, who was so big, never passed him without mocking words, and his brothers and sisters, who would not have noticed any difference unless it had been put into their heads, soon became as rude and unkind as the rest.

At last he could bear it no longer, and one day he fancied he saw signs of his mother turning against him too; so that night, when the ducks and hens were still asleep, he stole away through an open door, and under cover of the burdock leaves scrambled on by the bank of the canal, till he reached a wide grassy moor, full of soft marshy places where the reeds grew. Here he lay down, but he was too tired and too frightened to fall asleep, and with the earliest peep of the Sun the reeds began to rustle, and he saw that he had blundered into a colony of wild ducks. But as he could not run away again he stood up and bowed politely.

'You are ugly,' said the wild ducks, when they had looked him well over; 'but, however, it is no business of ours, unless you wish to marry one of our daughters, and that we should not allow.' And the duckling answered that he had no idea of marrying anybody, and wanted nothing but to be left alone after his long journey.

So for two whole days he lay quietly among the reeds, eating such food as he could find, and drinking the water of the moorland pool, till he felt himself quite strong again. He wished he might stay where he was for ever, he was so comfortable and happy, away from everyone, with nobody to bite him and tell him how ugly he was.

He was thinking these thoughts, when two young ganders caught sight of him as they were having their evening splash among the reeds, looking for their supper.

'We are getting tired of this moor,' they said, 'and to-morrow we think of trying another, where the lakes are larger and the feeding better. Will you come with us?'

'Is it nicer than this?' asked the duckling doubtfully. And the words were hardly out of his mouth, when 'Pif! pah!' and the two new-comers were stretched dead beside him.

At the sound of the gun the wild ducks in the rushes flew into the air, and for a few minutes the firing continued.

Luckily for himself the duckling could not fly, and he floundered along through the water till he could hide himself amidst some tall ferns which grew in a hollow. But before he got there he met a huge creature on four legs, which he afterwards knew to be a dog, who stood and gazed at him with a long red tongue hanging out of his mouth. The duckling grew cold with terror, and tried to hide his head beneath his little wings; but the dog snuffed at him and passed on, and he was able to reach his place of shelter.

'I am too ugly even for a dog to eat,' said he to himself. 'Well, that is a great mercy.' And he curled himself up in the soft grass till the shots died away in the distance.

When all had been quiet for a long time, and there were only stars to see him, he crept out and looked about him.

He would never go near a pool again, never, thought he; and seeing that the moor stretched far away in the opposite direction from which he had come, he marched bravely on till he got to a small cottage, which seemed too tumbledown for the stones to hold together many hours longer. Even the door only hung upon one hinge, and as the only light in the room sprang from a tiny fire, the duckling edged himself cautiously in, and lay down under a chair close to the broken door, from which he could get out if necessary. But no one seemed to see him or smell him; so he spent the rest of the night in peace.

Now in the cottage dwelt an old woman, her cat, and a hen; and it was really they, and not she, who were masters of the house. The old woman, who passed all her days in spinning yarn, which she sold at the nearest town, loved both the cat and the hen as her own children, and never contradicted them in any way; so it was their grace, and not hers, that the duckling would have to gain.

It was only next morning, when it grew light, that they noticed their visitor, who stood trembling before them, with his eye on the door ready to escape at any moment. They did not, however, appear very fierce, and the duckling became less afraid as they approached him.

'Can you lay eggs?' asked the hen. And the duckling answered meekly:

'No; I don't know how.' Upon which the hen turned her back, and the cat came forward.

'Can you ruffle your fur when you are angry, or purr when you are pleased?' said she. And again the duckling had to admit that he could do nothing but swim, which did not seem of much use to anybody.

So the cat and the hen went straight off to the old woman, who was still in bed.

'Such a useless creature has taken refuge here,' they said. 'It calls itself a duckling; but it can neither lay eggs nor purr! What had we better do with it?'

'Keep it, to be sure!' replied the old woman briskly. 'It is all nonsense about it not laying eggs. Anyway, we will let it stay here for a bit, and see what happens.'

So the duckling remained for three weeks, and shared the food of the cat and the hen; but nothing in the way of eggs happened at all. Then the Sun came out, and the air grew soft, and the duckling grew tired of being in a hut, and wanted with all his might to have a swim. And one morning he got so restless that even his friends noticed it.

'What is the matter?' asked the hen; and the duckling told her.

'I am so longing for the water again. You can't think how delicious it is to put your head under the water and dive straight to the bottom.'

'I don't think I should enjoy it,' replied the hen doubtfully. 'And I don't think the cat would like it either.' And the cat, when asked, agreed there was nothing she would hate so much.

'I can't stay here any longer, I Must get to the water,' repeated the duck. And the cat and the hen, who felt hurt and offended, answered shortly:

'Very well then, go.'

The duckling would have liked to say good-bye, and thank them for their kindness, as he was polite by nature; but they had both turned their backs on him, so he went out of the rickety door feeling rather sad. But, in spite of himself, he could not help a thrill of joy when he was out in the air and water once more, and cared little for the rude glances of the creatures he met. For a while he was quite happy and content; but soon the winter came on, and snow began to fall, and everything to grow very wet and uncomfortable. And the duckling soon found that it is one thing to enjoy being in the water, and quite another to like being damp on land.

The Sun was setting one day, like a great scarlet globe, and the river, to the duckling's vast bewilderment, was getting hard and slippery, when he heard a sound of whirring wings, and high up in the air a flock of swans were flying. They were as white as snow which had fallen during the night, and their long necks with yellow bills were stretched southwards, for they were going—they did not quite know whither—but to a land where the Sun shone all day. Oh, if he only could have gone with them! But that was not possible, of course; and besides, what sort of companion could an ugly thing like him be to those beautiful beings? So he walked sadly down to a sheltered pool and dived to the very bottom, and tried to think it was the greatest happiness he could dream of. But, all the same, he knew it wasn't!

And every morning it grew colder and colder, and the duckling had hard work to keep himself warm. Indeed, it would be truer to say that he never was warm at all; and at last, after one bitter night, his legs moved so slowly that the ice crept closer and closer, and when the morning light broke he was caught fast, as in a trap; and soon his senses went from him.

A few hours more and the poor duckling's life had been ended.

But, by good fortune, a man was crossing the river on his way to his work, and saw in a moment what had happened. He had on thick wooden shoes, and he went and stamped so hard on the ice that it broke, and then he picked up the duckling and tucked him under his sheepskin coat, where his frozen bones began to thaw a little.

Instead of going on his work, the man turned back and took the bird to his children, who gave him a warm mess to eat and put him in a box by the fire, and when they came back from school he was much more comfortable than he had been since he had left the old woman's cottage. They were kind little children, and wanted to play with him; but, alas! the poor fellow had never played in his life, and thought they wanted to tease him, and flew straight into the milk-pan, and then into the butter-dish, and from that into the meal-barrel, and at last, terrified at the noise and confusion, right out of the door, and hid himself in the snow amongst the bushes at the back of the house.

He never could tell afterwards exactly how he had spent the rest of the winter. He only knew that he was very miserable and that he never had enough to eat. But by-and-by things grew better. The earth became softer, the Sun hotter, the birds sang, and the flowers once more appeared in the grass. When he stood up, he felt different, somehow, from what he had done before he fell asleep among the reeds to which he had wandered after he had escaped from the peasant's hut. His body seemed larger, and his wings stronger. Something pink looked at him from the side of a hill. He thought he would fly towards it and see what it was.

Oh, how glorious it felt to be rushing through the air, wheeling first one way and then the other! He had never thought that flying could be like that! The duckling was almost sorry when he drew near the pink cloud and found it was made up of apple blossoms growing beside a cottage whose garden ran down to the banks of the canal. He fluttered slowly to the ground and paused for a few minutes under a thicket of syringas, and while he was gazing about him, there walked slowly past a flock of the same beautiful birds he had seen so many months ago. Fascinated, he watched them one by one step into the canal, and float quietly upon the waters as if they were part of them.

'I will follow them,' said the duckling to himself; 'ugly though I am, I would rather be killed by them than suffer all I have suffered from cold and hunger, and from the ducks and fowls who should have treated me kindly.' And flying quickly down to the water, he swam after them as fast as he could.

It did not take him long to reach them, for they had stopped to rest in a green pool shaded by a tree whose branches swept the water. And directly they saw him coming some of the younger ones swam out to meet him with cries of welcome, which again the duckling hardly understood. He approached them glad, yet trembling, and turning to one of the older birds, who by this time had left the shade of the tree, he said:

'If I am to die, I would rather you should kill me. I don't know why I was ever hatched, for I am too ugly to live.' And as he spoke, he bowed his head and looked down into the water.

Reflected in the still pool he saw many white shapes, with long necks and golden bills, and, without thinking, he looked for the dull grey body and the awkward skinny neck. But no such thing was there. Instead, he beheld beneath him a beautiful white swan!

'The new one is the best of all,' said the children when they came down to feed the swans with biscuit and cake before going to bed. 'His feathers are whiter and his beak more golden than the rest.'

And when he heard that, the duckling thought that it was worth while having undergone all the persecution and loneliness that he had passed through, as otherwise he would never have known what it was to be really happy.

Taken from Lang, A. (ed.) (1906) *The Orange Fairy Book*, **London: Longmans, Green and Co. at sacred-texts.com**

The shift that takes place in this tale is one of perception as the "ugly duckling" comes to realize that he is in fact a swan, and not an ugly duckling after all. Sometimes a shift in perception is all that is required to put all the apparent wrongs in our world to right. The secret lies in finding the key to facilitate the shift.

One way of bringing about a shift is by letting go of the old to allow the new to enter our lives, and this can be achieved by building a Death Doll.

Making a Death Doll is a Native American practice which enables you to leave your past behind, not by escaping from it but by recognizing it no longer serves you and letting it go.. The process entails making a doll to which you attach all your pain. As you find suitable objects to represent your concerns, you bring those objects to the pain in your body. The idea is to push your pain into the object, then attach it to the place on the doll that seems most appropriate. When the doll is complete, it is then ceremonially buried, leaving you free to start a new life cycle. Then you can set about building your Lifedoll, to represent the dreams you hope to turn into reality. The Lifedoll is an object for you to keep and cherish as it represents your preferred scenario.

Deathdoll

I've made you so many times before
And no doubt I'll make you again
For however often I bury you
Your return is as inevitable as the tide on to the shore
You rise to the surface from a hidden source
Seemingly inexhaustible

And what we are conscious of
Is merely the tip of the iceberg
Deathdoll
Let me nail my pain to you
Decorate you with my suffering
Mark you with my scars
Deathdoll
Let me transform you into this self that no longer serves me
To purge myself of the growth that is eating away at me
And sapping my life force
Then let me give you a suitable burial
And leave you behind me
Ready for a new beginning
And another fresh start

References

Tatar, Maria (2008). *The Annotated Hans Christian Andersen.* W. Norton & Company. pp. 99–118.

Bredsdorff, Elias (1975). *Hans Christian Andersen: The Story of his Life and Work* (1805-1875). Phaidon. ISBN 0-7148-1636-1.

Chisholm, Anne (2006-06-05). "The tale of an ugly duckling". *The Daily Telegraph.*

Shape-shifting to find a Mate

Apart from all being American Indian tales, what the stories that follow all shape in common is that in each case the shape-shifting that takes place is purposeful, with the intention of the shape-shifter being to find a mate.

The Bear Who Married a Woman
Tsimshian

Once upon a time there lived a widow of the tribe of the Gispaxlâ'ts. Many men tried to marry her daughter, but she declined them all.

The mother said, "When a man comes to marry you, feel of the palms of his hands. If they are soft, decline him. If they are rough, accept him." She meant that she wanted to have for a son-in-law a man skillful in building canoes.

Her daughter obeyed her commands and refused the wooings of all young men. One night a youth came to her bed. The palms of his hands were very rough, and therefore she accepted his suit. Early in the morning, however, he had suddenly disappeared, even before she had seen him.

When her mother arose early in the morning and went out, she found a halibut on the beach in front of the house, although it was midwinter. The following evening the young man came back, but disappeared again before the dawn of the day. In the morning the widow found a seal in front of the house. Thus they lived for some time. The young woman never saw the face of her husband; but every morning she found an animal on the beach, every day a larger one. Thus the widow came to be very rich.

She was anxious to see her son-in-law, and one day she waited until he arrived. Suddenly she saw a red bear emerge from the water. He carried a whale on each side, and put them down on the beach. As soon as he noticed that he was observed, he was transformed into a rock, which may be seen up to this day. He was a supernatural being of the sea.

Source: Franz Boas, Tsimshian Mythology (Washington, DC: United States Government Printing Office, 1916), p. 19.

The Tsimshian Indians are native to the coastal regions of British Columbia and southern Alaska.

The Girl Who Married the Crow
Thompson (Ntlakyapamuk)

A girl belonging to a village of four underground lodges near Lytton refused all suitors who had come from Spences Bridge, Nicola, Kamloops, and Lillooet, although they brought as marriage gifts robes, dentalia, and other valuables. Her parents and the chief of the village were angry with her for refusing so many good suitors. Therefore she became sad, and would have committed suicide had not her brothers talked kindly with her.

One morning, when she had gone to the river to bathe and to draw water for the house, she thought, "I wish a man from far away would come and take me!"

Crow-Man, who lived at the mouth of the river, heard her. He

SHAPE-SHIFTERS AND THEIR STORIES 63

said, "A pretty girl far away wants a husband. I wish I could go to her!"

At once a man appeared to him and said, "I will help you, if you will do as I direct you. You must shut your eyes and pray to me, and I shall grant your desire. Now begin!"

Crow-Man knelt down and prayed that he might be enabled to go to the girl. His eyes closed while he was praying. Then his helper told him to open his eyes and look at himself. He saw that he had been transformed into a crow, with wings and with black feathers all over his body. He was afraid, and remained silent.

His helper told him that he would not be a crow always, but only for the journey to the girl. He said, "Now, fly up the river! And early in the morning you will see a girl bathing near four underground lodges. She is the wife that you desire!"

It was springtime, when crows come up the river. Three mornings the girl had repeated her supplication for a husband. Early the fourth morning she went to the accustomed place, put down her bark water baskets, took off her clothes, and went to bathe. She had just made her supplication when a crow came up the river and passed close to her head.

She called him nasty names and said, "Why do you fly so close to my head, you black ugly bird? You will blind me with the dirt of your feet."

It was Crow-Man, who was acting under the instructions of his helper. He flew past out of sight, alighted on the ground, shut his eyes, and prayed. When he opened his eyes, he was a man again. He walked back to where the girl was washing herself in the water, and sat down on her clothes. Presently she saw him, and asked him to leave. She pleaded with him to go away, but he paid no heed.

When she had asked him four times, he replied, "If you will become my wife, I will release your clothes."

She assented, saying, "You must be my husband, for you have seen my naked body."

Crow-Man shut his eyes and prayed. When he opened them again, a large beaverskin robe was there, and a dugout cedar canoe. He gave the robe to his wife. They embarked in the canoe and went downstream.

As the girl did not return, the people looked for her. They found her clothes and the water baskets, and thought that she had drowned herself.

She lived in her husband's country for a while, and bore a son to him. When the boy was growing up, he wished to see his grandparents. Every day he asked for them. Finally his parents determined to take him to see them.

They went up the river in a canoe loaded with presents of many kinds, and eventually reached Lytton. They moored their canoe at the watering place. The weather was warm, and the woman's parents were living in a mat tent. Her younger sister came down to draw water and discovered them. She went back with the news; and the parents cleaned their house, and made ready to receive their son-in-law. He gave his father-in-law all the presents, and the people danced to welcome them. He made up his mind to live there and became an adopted member of the tribe.

Source: Franz Boas, *Folk-Tales of Salishan and Sahaptin Tribes* = Memoirs of the American Folklore Society, vol. 11 (Lancaster and New York: American Folklore Society, 1917), pp. 30-32.

This tale was collected by James A. Teit.

SHAPE-SHIFTERS AND THEIR STORIES 65

The place names mentioned in this legend (Lytton, Spences Bridge, Nicola, Kamloops, and Lillooet) are all in southern British Columbia. Lytton is at the junction of the Thompson and Fraser rivers.

The Woman Who Became a Horse
Skidi Pawnee

There was a village, and the men decided to go on a warpath. So these men started, and they journeyed for several days toward the south. They came to a thickly wooded country. They found wild horses, and among them was a spotted pony.

One man caught the spotted pony and took care of it. He took it home, and instructed his wife to look after it, as if it were their chief. This she did, and, further, she liked the horse very much. She took it where there was good grass. In the winter time she cut young cottonwood shoots for it, so that the horse was always fat. In the night, if it was stormy, she pulled a lot of dry grass, and when she put the blanket over the horse and tied it up, she stuffed the grass under the blanket, so the horse never got cold. It was always fine and sleek.

One summer evening she went to where she had tied the horse, and she met a fine-looking man, who had on a buffalo robe with a spotted horse pictured on it. She liked him; he smelt finely.

She followed him until they came to where the horse had been, and the man said, "You went with me. It is I who was a horse."

She was glad, for she liked the horse. For several years they were together, and the woman gave birth, and it was a spotted pony. When the pony was born, the woman found she had a tail like that of a horse. She also had long hair. When the colt sucked, the woman stood up.

For several years they roamed about, and had more ponies, all spotted. At home the man mourned for his lost wife. He could not make out why should go off.

People went on a hunt many years afterward, and they came across these spotted ponies. People did not care to attack them, for among them was a strange looking animal. But, as they came across them now and then, they decided to catch them. They were hard to catch, but at last they caught them, all but the woman, for she could run fast; but as they caught her children, she gave in and was caught.

People said, "This is the woman who was lost."

And some said, "No, it is not."

Her husband was sent for, and he recognized her. He took his bow and arrows out and shot her dead, for he did not like to see her with the horse's tail. The other spotted ponies were kept, and as they increased, they were spotted. So the people had many spotted ponies.

Source: George A. Dorsey, Traditions of the Skidi Pawnee = Memoirs of the American Folklore Society, vol. 8 (Boston and New York: Published for the American Folklore Society by Houghton, Mifflin, and Company, 1904), pp. 294-295.

The Bear Woman
Okanagon

It was late fall, and people were in the mountains hunting. Six people were living together: a man and his wife, his parents, and his two sisters.

One day when out hunting, the man came on a patch of lily roots. On his return home he said to his wife, "I saw a fine patch of large lilies. Tomorrow morning we shall move there and stay for a few days, so that you can dig them."

They set up a lodge near the place. And on the following morning early, on his way to hunt, he showed his wife the place and left her there to dig.

In the afternoon a large grizzly bear appeared at the place. The woman was intent on her work and did not notice the bear until he was close to her. He said to her, "I want you to be my wife."

She agreed, for she knew he would kill her if she refused. He took her on his back and carried her to his house.

Towards evening the hunter returned carrying a load of deer meat. His wife was not there. He thought, "She is late and will come soon."

He roasted meat for both of them. He ate, and then took his bow and arrows and went in search of his wife. He saw where she had been digging roots. He called, but received no answer. It grew dark, and he returned to his camp. He could not sleep. At daybreak he went out again. He saw the tracks of the grizzly bear going away, but no tracks of his wife leaving the spot. He thought she might have gone to his parents' camp, or the bear might have killed her, but he saw neither her tracks nor signs of a struggle with the bear.

He went to the camp. His father told him that she had not arrived. He related what he had seen, and his father said, "The grizzly bear has not killed her. He has married her."

The man could neither sleep nor eat. At last the fourth night he slept, for he was very tired.

His wife appeared to him in a dream and said, "The grizzly has taken me." She told him where the bear's house was. She said, "Every morning at daybreak he takes me to dig roots at a certain place. If you are strong, you can kill him; but he is very fierce and endowed with magic power. You must fix your arrows as I direct you, and sit where I tell you. I have prepared a hiding place for you, where you may sit on a boulder. Prepare medicine to wash me with, for otherwise, when the bear dies, I shall die too through his power. If he kills you, I shall kill myself. Get young fir-tops and konêlps [veratrum californicum, durand], and soak them in water. With these you must rub me. Prepare one arrow by rubbing it with fat of snakes, and the other arrow anoint with rattlesnake poison. Sit down on the rock in the place that I have prepared; and on the fourth morning, when I bring the bear past close to the rock, shoot him in the throat."

The hunter prepared everything as directed. He made two new arrows with detachable foreshafts. He made them very carefully, and put good stone heads on them. He searched for snakes, and anointed the foreshafts of his arrows and the points. Early in the morning he was at the place indicated.

The grizzly bear's house was a cave in a cliff, and at daybreak the man saw the smoke from his fire coming out through a hole in the top of the cliff. Soon he saw his wife and the bear emerge from the entrance. Her face was painted, and she carried her root digger. She dug roots, and the bear gathered them.

The man returned home and told what he had seen to his father, who said, "I have a strong guardian spirit, and I shall protect you. Do not be afraid. Act according the directions your wife has given to you in your dream, and kill the bear."

On the fourth morning at daybreak he was sitting on the rock. His wife and the bear drew near. She was digging in circles, and the grizzly bear followed her. When she made the fourth circle, she passed quite close to the rock.

He aimed an arrow at his wife, and she cried, "Husbands never kill their wives!" He lowered his bow and laughed.

The bear stood up and was angry. He abused the woman, calling her bad names. Just then he was close to the rock. The hunter spoke to him, and the bear turned to look at the hunter, who shot him right in the throat. The grizzly bear tried to pull out the arrow, but could remove only the shaft. He rushed at the hunter, but could not reach him. The hunter shot his second arrow with such great force that the shaft fell off. The bear fell over and died.

Then his wife swooned, and would have died through the bear's power, had not her husband rubbed her with fir-tops and veratrum.

She revived and stood up. She said, "I warn you not to have connection with me. The influence of the bear is still over me. Build a lodge of fir brush for me some distance away from the people. Let your sisters feed me, and wash me with fir and veratrum leaves. You may speak to me from a distance. Next spring, when the snow is almost gone, I shall be your wife again."

In the spring she washed at a stream, using hot water, and her sisters-in-law rubbed her with fir boughs. The hunter also washed. Then she went into his lodge, and lived with him as before.

Source: Franz Boas, Folk-Tales of Salishan and Sahaptin Tribes = Memoirs of the American Folklore Society, vol. 11 (Lancaster and New York: American Folklore Society, 1917), pp. 90-92.

This tale was collected by James A. Teit.

The Okanagon tribe belongs to the Salish group. Their territory included present-day British Columbia, northern Washington and Idaho, and western Montana.

The Fish-Man
Salish

Somewhere near the mouth of the Fraser River lived a girl who had refused all suitors.

After a while a man came to visit her, and lay with her at night.

The girl said to him, "You must stay until daylight, and show yourself to my parents."

He answered, "No, I am too poor. Your people would not like me."

As he continued to come every night, the girl told her parents, and they were very angry. Then Fish-Man caused the sea to recede for many miles from the village. He let all the freshwater streams dry up, and no rain fall. The animals became thirsty, and left the country. The people could get no fish, no game, and no water to drink.

The girl told the people, "My lover has done this, because you were wroth with him and refused him."

Then the people made a long walk of planks over the mud to the edge of the sea. At the end of this they built a large platform of planks, which they covered with mats. They heaped many woolen blankets on it. Then they dressed the girl in a fine robe, combed and oiled her hair, painted her face, and put down on her head. Then they placed her on the top of the blankets and left her there. At once the sky became overcast, rain fell, the springs burst out, the streams ran, and the sea came in. The people watched until the sea rose, and floated the platform with the blankets. They saw a man climb up beside the girl.

They stood up; and the girl called, "Now all is well. I shall visit you soon."

Night came on, and they saw them no more. In two days she came back, and told the people, "I live below the sea, in the fish country. The houses there are just the same as here, and the people live in the same way."

She returned again with her husband bringing presents of fish. She said, "Henceforth people here shall always be able to catch plenty of fish."

Once more she came to show them her newly born child. After that she returned to the sea, and was never seen again.

Source: Franz Boas, Folk-Tales of Salishan and Sahaptin Tribes = Memoirs of the American Folklore Society, vol. 11 (Lancaster and New York: American Folklore Society, 1917), p. 131.

This tale was collected by James A. Teit.

A note by Teit concerning his source: "This myth ... I collected at Hope [on the Fraser River], where interior influence is rather strong. Similar versions are said to be current among the Spuzzum Indians. The narrator was an old man who could speak some Thompson. The Fraser River flows through British Columbia, Canada, into the Strait of Georgia at the site of present-day Vancouver.

The Dark Skinned Man

The *Dark-skinned Man* is a folktale from Svaneti in the Republic of Georgia, translated by Ketevan Kalandadze. The formulaic opening, "There was and yet there was not", is the Georgian equivalent of our "Once upon a time". The observation that someone "walked a lot or walked little" is also frequently found in such tales.

Again and again in stories "...we see how things appear in threes: how things have to happen three times, how the hero is given three wishes; how Cinderella goes to the ball three times; how the hero or the heroine is the third of three children." (Booker, 2004, p.229). But why does the triad, a group or series consisting of three items, feature over and over again in folk-tales and legends, wherever they may originate from? The answer is that it has long been of significance for a number of reasons, some of which are listed below:

Photius, who was Patriarch of Constantinople from 858 to 867 and from 877 to 886, observed that the triad is the first odd number in energy, is the first perfect number and is a middle and analogy, and the Pythagoreans referred it to physiology, the cause of all that has the triple dimension. It was also believed to be the cause of good counsel, intelligence and knowledge, and a mistress of music, mistress also of geometry, possessing authority in whatever pertains to astronomy and the nature and knowledge of the heavenly bodies, connecting and leading them into effects. Every virtue was also believed to be suspended from it, and to proceed from it. It was also known as a "Middle and Analogy," because all comparisons consist of three terms, at least; and analogies were called by the ancients "middles." Additionally, on account of the perfection of the triad, oracles were delivered from a tripod, as is related of the Oracle at Delphi.

Ezekiel xiv. v. 14 mentions three men who saw a creation, destruction and a restoration; Noah of the whole world, Daniel of the Jewish world Jerusalem and Job of his personal world.

There is also the Hindu Trinity of Brahma, consisting of Brahma, Vishnu and Siva; Creator, Preserver and Changer.

The Three Fates can be listed too - Clotho, Lachesis and Atropos. Then there are the Three Furies - Tisiphone, Alecto and Megæra. Mention can also be made of the Three Graces - Euphrosyne, Aglaia and Thalia. In addition, there are the Three Judges of Hades - Minos, Æacus and Rhadamanthus.

As for the Druids, their poems are noted as being composed in triads.

Then there is the transcendent importance of the Christian Trinity. In old paintings we often see a trinity of Jesus with John and Mary.

For the Jews, monograms of Jehovah were triple; thus three rays and the Shin, and three yods in a triangle.

In the Timæus of Plato, the Divine Triad is called Theos: God; Logos, the Word and Psyche, the Soul. Indeed it is impossible to study any single system of worship throughout the world, without being struck by the peculiar persistence of the triple number in regard to divinity; whether as a group of deities, a triformed or three-headed god, a Mysterious Triunity, a deity of three powers, or a family relationship of three Persons, such as the Father, Mother and Son of the Egyptians, Osiris, Isis and Horus.

Three is a notable number in the mythology of the Norseman too: the great Ash-tree Yggdrasil supported the world. It had three roots; one extended into Asgard, the abode of the Gods; one into Jotenheim, the home of the Giants, and the third into Nifleheim, the region of the Unknown. The three Norns (Fates) attend to the root in Asgard: they were Urda (the past); Verdandi (the present) and Skulda (the future).

The Talmuds are crowded with quaint conceits concerning the triad, and many are very curious:- He who three times daily repeats the 114th Psalm is sure of future happiness; Three precious gifts were given to the Jews - the Law of Moses, the Land of Israel and Paradise; In three sorts of dreams there is truth; the last dream of the morning, the dream which is also dreamed by a neighbour, and a dream twice repeated; Three things calm a man; melody, scenery and sweet scent: and three things improve a man; a fine house, a handsome wife and good furniture; Three despise their fellows; cooks, fortune-tellers and dogs; Three love their fellows; proselytes, slaves and ravens; Three persons live a life which is no life; he who lives at another man's table, he who is ruled by his wife, and he who is incapable from bodily affliction.

Then there are three keys which God keeps to himself, and which no man can gain nor use; the key of life, the key of rain and the key of the resuscitation of the dead. Taanith, 2; 1 and 2; The Jewish butcher of Kosher meat must use three knives; one to slaughter the animal, another to cut it up and a third to remove the suet, which it is forbidden to eat; Three acolytes had to attend the High Priest when he went in to worship; one at his right, one at his left, and one had to hold up the gems on the train of his vestment.

Among the Brahmins there were three great Vedas; three Margas or ways of salvation; three Gunas, the Satva, quiescence; Rajas, desire; and Tamas, decay. Three Lokas - Swarga, Bhumi and Patala;

heaven, earth and hell. Three Jewels of wisdom, the Tri-ratnas; Buddha, Dharma and Sanga. The three Fires are the three aspects of the human soul - Atma, Buddhi and Manas. There were three prongs of the trident, and three eyes in the forehead of Siva. Note also the three-syllabled holy word AUM.

At the Oblation of the Elements in the Celtic Church, three drops of wine and three drops of water were poured into the chalice. And in the present Christian Church we notice three crossings with water at Baptism, three Creeds, the Banns of Marriage are published three times and a Bishop in benediction makes the Sign of the Cross three times. In Roman Catholic churches, the Angelus Bell is rung three times a day, a peal of three times three for the heavenly hierarchies of angels: Pope John XXII ordered that the faithful should say three Aves on each occasion.

Last but not least, mention should be made of the I Ching or Book of Changes, one of the oldest of the Chinese classic texts, as it contains a divination system based on triads. The standard text originated from the ancient text (古文經) transmitted by Fei Zhi (費直 , c50 BCE - CE 10) of the Han Dynasty. Each hexagram represents a description of a state or process and is composed of four three-line arrangements called trigrams, of which there are eight:— khien, tui, li, chan, sien, khan, kan and kwan; each expressed by figures of one long and two short lines. (Adapted from The Triad in Westcott, 1911, pp. 41-48).

There is also The Threefold Law (a.k.a. the Law of Return) in the Wiccan Rede, an ethical code for witches, which adds a reward for those who follow the code, and a punishment for those who violate it. The law states that "All good that a person does to another returns three fold in this life; harm is also returned three fold."

Apart from the focus on the number three, water also plays an important part in this story. The Waters have been described as the reservoir of all the potentialities of existence because they not only precede every form but they also serve to sustain every creation. Immersion is equivalent to dissolution of form, in other words death, whereas emergence repeats the cosmogonic act of formal manifestation, in other words re-birth (see Eliade, 1952, p.151). And, following on from this, the surface of water can be defined as "the meeting place and doorway from one realm to another: from that which is revealed to that which is hidden, from conscious to unconscious" (Shaw & Francis, 2008, p.13).

Water in pre-historic times was seen to be the source of all life, but culturally we have lost this sacred connection. Water is the matrix, a deep and ancient force, and we are all born of the primordial waters. We grow within a maternal embryonic sac, and water makes up most of our bodily composition so we are physically linked (Greenwood, 2012, p.63).

This creative power of water is reflected in Norse mythology, among others. The Elivagar are eleven rivers that exist in Ginnungagap, the primeval void that arises from Hvergelmir a bubbling boiling spring in the cold realm of Niflheim. From the meeting of the ice from these frozen rivers and fire from Muspellheim, the fiery realm, water is created. From water the cosmos is formed. Such is the importance of water in this creation story (Greenwood, 2012, p.59).

Not only does water create life though. It is by passing through water forms can change, just as the dark-skinned man changes in this particular story.

The journey to another reality frequently involves passing through some kind of gateway. As Eliade explains,

The "clashing of rocks," the "dancing reeds," the gates in the shape of jaws, the "two razor-edged restless mountains," the "two clashing icebergs," the "active door," the "revolving barrier," the door made of the two halves of the eagle's beak, and many more – all these are images used in myths and sagas to suggest the insurmountable difficulties of passage to the Other World (Eliade, 2003, pp.64-65).

In this tale, the white lake acts as this gateway. By making the choice to pass through it, the dark-skinned man is able to effect his transformation, but is unable to fully control the form it takes. However, everything works out for the best in the end, and the equilibrium of the community is restored once again with the marriage of his three sons to the three princesses, a trinity of trinities.

Finally, let us consider the androgyny of the dark-skinned man, at least his repeated transition from one sex to another. As Joan Halifax observes, the dissolution of opposites, such as life and death or male and female, and the subsequent "making whole again" is one of the main features in the initiation and transformation process as experienced by the shaman, at least in the case of indigenous forms of shamanism (see Ripinsky-Naxon, 1993, pp.84-85).

According to the deconstructionists, polarities and privileged positions are simply arbitrary human constructions, and "objective reality" does not exist (see Hansen, 2001, p. 64). Shamans, and the dark-skinned man can be regarded as one, are master deconstructionalists. By consorting with spirits, for example, they regularly deconstruct the polarity of life and death. One can even argue it is essential for shamans to deconstruct order, especially if a person's or a community's rigidity of outlook have blocked adaptation and growth, and they need to view their situation in a new light in order to remove the impasse.

References

Ashliman, D.L. *Folklore and Mythology Electronic Texts* www.pitt.edu/~dash/folktexts.html (accessed 27/09/09)

Berman, M. (2010) *All God's Creatures*, California: Pendraig Publishing.

Booker, C. (2004) *The Seven Basic Plots: Why we tell Stories*, London: Continuum.

Eliade, M. (1991) *Images and Symbols*, New Jersey: Princeton University Press (The original edition is copyright Librairie Gallimard 1952).

Eliade, M. (2003) *Rites and Symbols of Initiation*, Putnam, Connecticut: Spring Publications (originally published by Harper Bros., New York, 1958).

Greenwood, S. (2012) 'The Dragon Waters of Place: A Journey to the Source' In MacLellan, G. & Cross, S. *The Wanton Green*, Mandrake of Oxford.

Hansen, G. P. (2001). *The Trickster and the Paranormal*, New York: Xlibris.

Perrault, C. (1921) *Old-Time Stories told by Master Charles Perrault*, translated by A. E. Johnson, New York: Dodd Mead and Company.

Rappoport, A.S. (1937) *The Folklore of the Jews*, London: The Soncino Press, 1937. No copyright notice.

Ripinsky-Naxon, M. (1993) *The Nature of Shamanism*, Albany: State University of New York Press.

Shaw, S. & Francis, A. (eds.) (2008) *Deep Blue: Critical reflections on Nature, Religion and Water*, London: Equinox Publishing Ltd.

The Dark-skinned Man

There was and yet there was not, there were a husband and a wife. They loved each other dearly and you could even say they were each other's Sun and Moon. Because of his dark skin everyone used to call the husband a dark man, and this led to him to always asking his wife the same question, over and over again:

"So what do you think – I'm a good man, aren't I?"

And the woman always had the same answer:

"Yes, you are, my dark man but... - and then she would never finish the sentence."

One day the dark man insisted on her finishing the sentence. So she said:

"You are certainly a good man, but to be honest, it would have been better if you didn't have such dark skin."

"Not to worry because I'm going to deal with that problem," the dark man said. He couldn't do anything that day, but next day he got up very early, at the crack of dawn, prepared a packed lunch for himself and left. He walked a lot or he walked little, until finally he came to a white lake where he decided to have a break because he was very tired by then.

Suddenly, from out of nowhere, a blackbird appeared. It dived into the lake from the side where the man was resting and then emerged from the other side of the lake as white as snow.

"What good fortune!" The dark-skinned man shouted with joy. "I'll jump into this water right now and, with a bit of luck, I'll emerge from it just as white as that blackbird did.

So he took his clothes off and dived into the water. However, he emerged from it on the other side of the lake, not as a man but as a white-skinned woman.

The dark-skinned man of course would have preferred to stay dark and be a man, but there was nothing at all he could do about it and just had to accept his fate. In the meantime, the king's hunters had come to the lake and when they saw how beautiful the white-skinned woman was, they captured her and took her to the king. The king's son liked the woman very much and married her. The dark-skinned man, now a white-skinned woman, lived with the prince for three years and gave birth to three sons.

As time passed, the white-skinned woman, not surprisingly started to ask herself what she was doing there. "Whose children am I bringing up? I have to do something about this." So she went back to the white lake again, jumped into it again, but emerged on the other side of it as a white mare this time. The mare had no sooner emerged from the water than the king's hunters seized her and placed her in the king's stable. Every single male horse was after her. Of course the dark-skinned man would have preferred to remain a woman rather than be a mare, but once again there was nothing he could do about the situation. He spent 3 years among the horses and gave birth to three striking foals. Finally the time came when she started to question what she was doing there. "Whose offspring am I bringing up? I have to do something about this." So the mare went back to the white lake again, jumped into the water, and this time came out of it on the other side as a white bitch.

The king's hunters came, grabbed hold of her and took her to join the other dogs in the king's pack. Every single male dog was after her. Of course the dark-skinned man would have preferred to remain a mare rather than be a dog, but once again there was nothing he could do about it, and the bitch gave birth to three male puppies. Finally she asked herself: what she was doing there. "Whose children am I bringing up? I have to do something about this." So the bitch went back to the white lake again, jumped into the water, and emerged from it as a dark-skinned man once again. He found his old clothes lying on the bank, got dressed, and carried on walking. He walked a lot or he walked little until he came to a different kingdom. He heard that the king there had three daughters and he wanted to marry them off, but on one condition. The bride's husband-to-be had to boil the water in a huge saucepan, but without a fire. Three huge saucepans were placed outside the king's palace for the purpose and a large crowd of people gathered to see the challenge take place.

The dark-skinned man decided to have a go and headed towards the palace with that aim in mind. But he came to a river without a bridge. A horse man was passing by and the dark-skinned man asked him for help, but the horse man didn't even look at him. A second horse man passed by but he also refused to take the dark-skinned man across. Finally, a third horse man did agree to take him to the other side of the river. The dark-skinned man walked and walked until he came to the palace. There he found a massive crowd of people gathered around the saucepans. Despite all their efforts though, none of them had been able to boil the water in them yet. The dark-skinned man tried to sneak through the crowd, but he couldn't. At that point, the king himself saw the dark-skinned man and told his servants to let the stranger have a try. "Who knows? Everybody else has failed but he might be lucky!"

The dark-skinned man went up to the first saucepan and started to tell his first story: he spoke of how he came to the white lake and turned into a white-skinned woman there, how he was captured and taken to the king's palace where he married the prince, about the three sons they had and how he spent three years bringing them up. He didn't leave out a single detail of what he had been through during that time. And from the sadness of the dark man's story the water in the first saucepan started to boil!

Then he approached the second saucepan and started to tell his second story. He talked about how he went back to the white lake once again, how he jumped in it and emerged on the other side as a white mare, how he was captured and placed in the king's stable, how he gave birth to three striking foals and how he then spent three years raising them. He told the saucepan absolutely everything, right down to the last detail. And from the sadness of the dark man's story, the water in the second saucepan started to boil!

Finally, he came to the third saucepan and started to tell his third story. He talked about how he came to the white lake for the third time, jumped into it and came out as a white bitch, how he was captured by the king's hunters, how he was placed in a pack with the other dogs belonging to the king, how he gave birth to three male puppies while he was there, and strange it had felt to be bringing up someone else's children. When he eventually finished telling his tale, from the sadness of his story the water in the third saucepan started to boil!

The king had to keep his promise so the dark-skinned man was given the three daughters. So he took them and married them to his three sons. Then he went and found his wife and they lived together happily ever after.

May you live a long and happy life before you eventually go to meet them! God bless you.

Humans with animal ears or horns: If only I could be something else

In its broadest sense, shape-shifting occurs when a being (usually human) either (1) has the ability to change its shape into that of another person, creature, or other entity or (2) finds its shape involuntarily changed by someone else. If the shape change is voluntary, its cause may be an act of will, a magic word or magic words, a potion, or a magic object. If the change is involuntary, its cause may be a curse or spell, a wizard's or magician's or fairy's help, a deity's will, a temporal change such as a full Moon or nightfall, love, or death. The transformation may or may not be purposeful.

Therianthropy refers to the metamorphosis of humans into other animals, and therianthropes are said to change forms via shape-shifting. What the characters in this Chapter all have in common is that their transformations are not only involuntary but also incomplete. Consequently, they are neither human nor animal, but a mixture of both. It is a problem they attempt to address in a variety of different ways, though the only solution to their plights, as they eventually discover for themselves, is to come to terms with who they are.

The Goat's Ears of the Emperor Trojan
Serbia

Once upon a time there lived an emperor whose name was Trojan, and he had ears like a goat. Every morning, when he was shaved, he asked if the man saw anything odd about him, and as each fresh barber always replied that the emperor had goat's ears, he was at once ordered to be put to death.

Now after this state of things had lasted a good while, there was hardly a barber left in the town that could shave the emperor, and it came to be the turn of the Master of the Company of Barbers to go up to the palace. But, unluckily, at the very moment that he should have set out, the master fell suddenly ill, and told one of his apprentices that he must go in his stead.

When the youth was taken to the emperor's bedroom, he was asked why he had come and not his master. The young man replied that the master was ill, and there was no one but himself who could be trusted with the honor. The emperor was satisfied with the answer, and sat down, and let a sheet of fine linen be put round him.

Directly the young barber began his work, he, like the rest, remarked the goat's ears of the emperor, but when he had finished and the emperor asked his usual question as to whether the youth had noticed anything odd about him, the young man replied calmly, "No, nothing at all."

This pleased the emperor so much that he gave him twelve ducats, and said, "Henceforth you shall come every day to shave me."

So when the apprentice returned home, and the master inquired how he had got on with the emperor, the young man answered, "Oh, very well, and he says I am to shave him every day, and he has given me these twelve ducats"; but he said nothing about the goat's ears of the emperor.

From this time the apprentice went regularly up to the palace, receiving each morning twelve ducats in payment. But after a while, his secret, which he had carefully kept, burnt within him, and he longed to tell it to somebody. His master saw there was something on his mind, and asked what it was. The youth replied that he had been tormenting himself for some months, and should never feel easy until someone shared his secret.

"Well, trust me," said the master, "I will keep it to myself; or, if you do not like to do that, confess it to your pastor, or go into some field outside the town and dig a hole, and, after you have dug it, kneel down and whisper your secret three times into the hole. Then put back the earth and come away."

The apprentice thought that this seemed the best plan, and that very afternoon went to a meadow outside the town, dug a deep hole, then knelt and whispered to it three times over, "The Emperor Trojan has goat's ears." And as he said so a great burden seemed to roll off him, and he shoveled the earth carefully back and ran lightly home.

Weeks passed away, and there sprang up in the hole an elder tree which had three stems, all as straight as poplars. Some shepherds, tending their flocks nearby, noticed the tree growing there, and one of them cut down a stem to make flutes of; but, directly he began to play, the flute would do nothing but sing: "The Emperor Trojan has goat's ears." Of course, it was not long before the whole town knew of this wonderful flute and what it said; and, at last, the news reached the emperor in his palace.

He instantly sent for the apprentice and said to him, "What have you been saying about me to all my people?"

The culprit tried to defend himself by saying that he had never told anyone what he had noticed; but the emperor, instead of listening, only drew his sword from its sheath, which so frightened the poor fellow that he confessed exactly what he had done, and how he had whispered the truth three times to the earth, and how in that very place an elder tree had sprung up, and flutes had been cut from it, which would only repeat the words he had said. Then the emperor commanded his coach to be made ready, and he took the youth with him, and they drove to the spot, for he wished to see for himself whether the young man's confession was true; but when they reached the place only one stem was left. So the emperor desired his attendants to cut him a flute from the remaining stem, and, when it was ready, he ordered his chamberlain to play on it. But no tune could the chamberlain play, though he was the best flute player about the court — nothing came but the words, "The Emperor Trojan has goat's ears."

Then the emperor knew that even the earth gave up its secrets, and he granted the young man his life, but he never allowed him to be his barber any more.

Source: Andrew Lang, The Violet Fairy Book (London: Longmans, Green, and Company, 1901), pp. 52-54.

The King with the Horse's Ears
Ireland

The story I'm going to tell you is not to be met every day. I heard little Tom Kennedy, the great schoolmaster of Rossard, say that he read it in the history of Ireland, and that it happened before the people were Christian. It is about a king who had his hair cut only once a year. He lived in some old city on the borders of Carlow and Kilkenny, and his name was a queer one: Lora Lonshach it was.

So, as I said, he got his hair cut only once a year, and afterward nothing more was ever heard of the barber who did it. This happened to about seven unlucky fellows, and then no barber would come close the castle for love or money. So the king proclaimed that all the barbers in the country were to draw lots, and if the one who got the short straw would dare to refuse, he would be put to death.

The short straw was drawn by a poor widow's son named Thigueen. Fearing that she would never again see her son, the mother ran to the castle and beseeched the king to spare him the fate of the previous barbers.

"You'll get your boy back safe and sound," promised the king.

The next day the frightened barber reported for duty.

"My good fellow," said the king, "you'll be at liberty to go wherever you please after cutting my hair, but you must swear Dar lamh an Righ (by the king's hand) that you'll never tell anything that has ears and tongue what you see here today."

The king sat down on his throne and took off his hood, revealing two brown horse's ears, quite as long as those of an ass.

"Pick up your scissors and do your job!" he ordered.

The poor lad did as best he could, taking special care not to nick the king's ears.

When the job was finished, the king paid him, saying, "Now, my lad, if I ever hear word of this, I'll make you wish that you had never been born."

The boy returned to his mother, only to fall into bed, deathly ill. She asked him what ailed him, but he gave no answer.

Two days later the doctor came.

"I have a secret," said poor Thigueen. "If I cannot tell it, I'll die, and if I do tell it, I'll not be allowed to live."

When the doctor heard that the secret was not to be told to anyone with a tongue or ears, he said, "Go into the woods, make a split in the bark of one of the trees, tell your secret into the cut."

The doctor was hardly out of the house when Thigueen got up and went into the woods, not stopping until he reached the middle, a place where two paths crossed one another. At this spot he found a healthy tree, cut a gash in its bark, and then whispered into it, "Da Chluais Chapail ar Labhradh Loingseach," which means, "The two ears of a horse has Lora Lonshach."

The poor fellow had hardly whispered these words when he felt as if a mountain had been lifted off his back.

Before a year passed, when again it would be time for the king's haircut, a great harp-playing match was announced, a contest between Craftine, the king's harper, and anyone who dared play against him. The other four kings of Ireland were invited, as well as all the lords and ladies who chose to travel so far. One week before the appointed day, Craftine found a crack in his harp, so he went into the forest to look for wood for a new one.

Where should bad luck send him but to the very tree that Thigueen had told his secret to! Craftine cut it down and fashioned it into the finest harp you have ever seen, and when he tried it, he himself was enchanted with its beautiful music.

The great day came at last, and the big hall in the palace was crammed. The king was on his high throne, with the four other kings before him. On either side were all the great lords and ladies, around the open place in the center where the harpers were sitting.

Craftine began. He first played so mournfully that all who heard him were grief-stricken. Then he played a merry jig, and because there was no room to dance, everyone shouted out for joy. Next came a war-like march, and everyone who had room drew his sword and waved it over his head, each one crying out the war-cry of his own chief or king. Finally he played a beautiful heavenly tune, and they all closed their eyes, hoping that the beautiful music would never come to an end.

When Craftine finally ceased playing, gold and silver were thrown in showers to him. Then the harpers of Leinster, Munster, Connaught, and Ulster tried their hands, and, sure enough, they played very well, but not nearly as well as Craftine.

When they were finished, the king said to Craftine, "Give us one more tune to finish decently, and put all that we invited in good humor for their dinner."

"I am afraid of my harp," answered Craftine. "It wasn't my fingers that struck out the music, but the music that stirred my fingers. There is magic in that harp, and I fear it will play us some trick."

"Trick be hanged!" said the king. "Play away!"

The harper had to obey his king, and he took up his harp, but he had hardly touched the strings, when a loud voice came from them, shouting, "Da Chluais Chapail ar Labhradh Loingseach!"

The startled king put his hands to his head, not knowing what he was doing, and in his fumbling he loosened the bands of his hood, revealing the two long hairy ears. What a roar came from the crowd! King Lora was not able to stand it, and in a trance he fell down from his throne. In a few minutes he had the hall to himself, except for his harper and some of his old servants.

They say that when he came to himself, he was very sorry for all the poor barbers that he had put out of the way, and that he pensioned their wives and mothers. From then on Thigueen was no more concerned about giving the king a haircut than he would have been about giving one to you or to me.

Source: Abstracted from Patrick Kennedy, *Legendary Fictions of the Irish Celts*, 2nd edition, London and New York: Macmillan and Company, (1891), pp. 219-225.

Many of us waste away large chunks of our lives trying to be someone or something else, and March ab Meirchion was no exception. Eventually though, he came to accept his fate and that is surely what we should all strive towards, for it is the only way we can ever truly be at peace with ourselves.

March's Ears
Wales

March ab Meirchion was lord of Castellmarch, in Lleyn. He ruled over leagues of rich land, tilled by hundreds of willing and obedient vassals. He had great possessions, fleet horses, greyhounds, hawks, countless black cattle and sheep, and a great herd of swine. (But few possessed pigs at that time, and their flesh was esteemed better than the flesh of oxen. Arthur himself sought to have one of March's sows.) In his palace he had much treasure of gold, silver, and Conway pearls, and all men envied him.

But March was not happy. He had a secret, and day and night he was torn with dread lest it should be discovered. He had horse's ears!

To no one was the secret known except his barber. This man he compelled to take a solemn oath that he would not reveal his deformity to any living soul. If he wittingly or unwittingly should let anyone know that March's ears were other than human, March swore that he would cut his head off.

The barber became as unhappy as March. Indeed his wretchedness was greater, because his fate would be worse if the secret were revealed. March would undergo ridicule, which is certainly a serious thing, but the barber would undergo decapitation, which is much more serious.

The secret disagreed with his constitution so violently that he lost his appetite and his colour, and began to fall into a decline.

So ill did he become that he had to call in a physician. This man was skilled in his craft, and he said to the barber, "You are being killed by a suppressed secret. Unless you communicate it to someone you will soon be in your grave."

This announcement did not give the barber much consolation. He explained to the physician that if he did as he was directed he would lose his head. If in any event he had to come to the end of his earthly career, he preferred being interred with his head joined to, rather than separated from, his trunk.

The physician then suggested that he should tell his secret to the ground.

The barber thought there was not much danger to his cervical vertebrae (this is the learned name for neck bones) if he did this, and adopted the suggestion. He was at once relieved. His colour and appetite gradually came back, and before long he was as strong and well as he had ever been.

Now it happened that a fine crop of reeds grew on the spot where the barber whispered his secret to the ground.

March prepared a great feast, and sent for one of Maelgwn

Gwynedd's pipers, who was the best piper in the world, to make music for his guests.

On his way to Castellmarch, the piper observed these fine reeds, and as his old pipe was getting worn out, he cut them and made an excellent new pipe. When his guests had eaten and drunk, March ordered the piper to play.

What was the surprise of all when the pipe gave out no music, but only the words, "Horse's ears for March ab Meirchion, horse's ears for March ab Meirchion," over and over again.

March drew his sword and would have slain the piper, but the hapless musician begged for mercy. He was not to blame, he said. He had tried to play his wonted music, but the pipe was charmed, and do what he would, he could get nothing out of it but the words, "Horse's ears for March ab Meirchion."

March tried the pipe himself, but even he could not elicit any strains from it, but only the words, "Horse's ears for March ab Meirchion."

So he forgave the piper and made no further effort to conceal his deformity.

Source: W. Jenkyn Thomas, *The Welsh Fairy Book,* London: T. Fisher Unwin Ltd. (1908), pp. 93-95.

It is not only frustrating to constantly strive to be someone you are not, it can also be extremely dangerous, and that is the lesson to be learnt from the penultimate tale in this Chapter:

The Three Wishes

ONCE upon a time, and be sure 'twas a long time ago, there lived a poor woodman in a great forest, and every day of his life he went out to fell timber. So one day he started out, and the goodwife filled his wallet and slung his bottle on his back, that he might have meat and drink in the forest. He had marked out a huge old oak, which, thought he, would furnish many and many a good plank. And when he was come to it, he took his axe in his hand and swung it round his head as though he were minded to fell the tree at one stroke. But he hadn't given one blow, when what should he hear but the pitifullest entreating, and there stood before him a fairy who prayed and beseeched him to spare the tree. He was dazed, as you may fancy, with wonderment and affright, and he couldn't open his mouth to utter a word. But he found his tongue at last, and, 'Well,' said he, 'I'll e'en do as thou wishest.'

'You've done better for yourself than you know,' answered the fairy, 'and to show I'm not ungrateful, I'll grant you your next three wishes, be they what they may.' And therewith the fairy was no more to be seen, and the woodman slung his wallet over his shoulder and his bottle at his side, and off he started home.

But the way was long, and the poor man was regularly dazed with the wonderful thing that had befallen him, and when he got home there was nothing in his noddle but the wish to sit down and rest. Maybe, too, 'twas a trick of the fairy's. Who can tell? Anyhow, down he sat by the blazing fire, and as he sat he waxed hungry, though it was a long way off supper-time yet.

'Hasn't thou naught for supper, dame?' said he to his wife.

'Nay, not for a couple of hours yet,' said she.

'Ah!' groaned the woodman, 'I wish I'd a good link of black pudding here before me.'

No sooner had he said the word, when clatter, clatter, rustle, rustle, what should come down the chimney but a link of the finest black pudding the heart of man could wish for.

If the woodman stared, the goodwife stared three times as much. 'What's all this?' says she.

Then all the morning's work came back to the woodman, and he told his tale right out, from beginning to end, and as he told it the goodwife glowered and glowered, and when he had made an end of it she burst out, 'Thou bee'st but a fool, Jan, thou bee'st but a fool; and I wish the pudding were at thy nose, I do indeed.'

And before you could say Jack Robinson, there the good man sat and his nose was the longer for a noble link of black pudding.

He gave a pull, but it stuck, and she gave a pull, but it stuck, and they both pulled till they had nigh pulled the nose off, but it stuck and stuck.

'What's to be done now?' said he.

'"Tisn't so very unsightly,' said she, looking hard at him.

Then the woodman saw that if he wished, he must need wish in a hurry; and wish he did, that the black pudding might come off his nose. Well! there it lay in a dish on the table, and if the goodman and goodwife didn't ride in a golden coach, or dress in silk and satin, why, they had at least as fine a black pudding for their supper as the heart of man could desire.

Taken from *More English Fairy Tales*, collected and edited by Joseph Jacobs. London, D. Nutt [1894]. Scanned and redacted by Phillip Brown. Additional proofing and formatting at sacred-texts.com by John B. Hare, April 2003. This text is in the public domain. These files may be used for any non-commercial purpose provided this notice of attribution is left intact.

The Chinese fable presented below reiterates the same message too:

The Stonecutter

There was once a stonecutter, who was dissatisfied with himself and with his position in life.

One day, he passed a wealthy merchant's house, and through the open gateway, saw many fine possessions and important visitors. "How powerful that merchant must be!" thought the stonecutter. He became very envious, and wished that he could be like the merchant. Then he would no longer have to live the life of a mere stonecutter.

To his great surprise, he suddenly became the merchant, enjoying more luxuries and power than he had ever dreamed of, envied and detested by those less wealthy than himself. But soon a high official passed by, carried in a sedan chair, accompanied by attendants, and escorted by soldiers beating gongs. Everyone, no matter how wealthy, had to bow low before the procession. "How powerful that official is!" he thought. "I wish that I could be a high official!"

Then he became the high official, carried everywhere in his embroidered sedan chair, feared and hated by the people all around, who had to bow down before him as he passed. It was a hot summer day, and the official felt very uncomfortable in the sticky sedan chair. He looked up at the Sun. It shone proudly in the sky, unaffected by his presence. "How powerful the Sun is!" he thought. "I wish that I could be the Sun!"

Then he became the sun, shining fiercely down on everyone, scorching the fields, cursed by the farmers and labourers. But a huge black cloud moved between him and the Earth, so that his light could no longer shine on everything below. "How powerful that storm cloud is!" he thought. "I wish that I could be a cloud!"

Then he became the cloud, flooding the fields and villages, shouted at by everyone. But soon he found that he was being pushed away by some great force, and realized that it was the wind. "How powerful it is!" he thought. "I wish that I could be the wind!"

Then he became the wind, blowing tiles off the roofs of houses, uprooting trees, hated and feared by all below him. But after a while, he ran up against something that would not move, no matter how forcefully he blew against it — a huge, towering stone. "How powerful that stone is!" he thought. "I wish that I could be a stone!" he thought. "I wish that I could be a stone!"

Then he became the stone, more powerful than anything else on Earth. But as he stood there, he heard the sound of a hammer pounding a chisel into the solid rock, and felt himself being changed. "What could be more powerful than I, the stone?" he thought. He looked down and saw far below him the figure of a stonecutter.

All Life is Connected and there is Life in Everything

One of the unique qualities of water is that it can exist in all three states - solid in the form of ice, liquid, and also as vapour.

It also provides the ideal medium for the shape-shifter as being submerged in it represents leaving this world behind and emerging from it is the equivalent of rebirth. What the following group of tales all share in common is that the transformation in each case is from the element of water itself into human form and then back again. And any happiness to be derived from the transformation is counterbalanced by the suffering that inevitably follows its reversal. Is the happiness worth all the pain that it leaves in its wake is a question that we have been asking ourselves since we first appeared on this Earth, and will more than likely long continue to ask. As for the answer, that is for each of us to determine for ourselves.

The Snow Maiden
Russia

Many years ago, in a distant Russian village, there lived a peasant, by name Akem, with his wife Masha; they lived in a small wooden hut, where they spent their days in love and harmony; but children had they none. This was a very sore point with both of them, they used to sit by the window or at the door of their little hut looking at their neighbours' children playing about, and wished that they had some of their own; but finding that it was no use wishing, they at last became sad in their old age.

One cold winter's day, when the snow lay thick upon the uneven country roads, and the little village boys were running about throwing snowballs to keep themselves warm, and making snowmen and women, old Akem and Masha sat by their window looking at them in silence. Suddenly Akem looked up at his wife, and said, laughing, "Masha, what do you say to coming out into the road and making ourselves a snowman or woman, like those little boys yonder?"

Masha laughed, too, it seemed such a queer thing to do at their time of life! "Yes, if you like," she replied; "let us go, it may cheer us up a bit; but I don't see why we should make a snowman or woman, let us rather make a child out of snow, as Providence does not seem to wish us to have a real one!"

"I do believe you are getting quite clever in your old age, Masha! Come along, then, and let us set to work."

Off went the old couple, laughing at themselves all the while, and sure enough they commenced making a snow child! They made the legs, arms, hands, feet, and a snowball for the head.

"What, in the name of wonder, are you up to?" exclaimed a passerby, stopping suddenly in front of the two old people.

"A snow child!" laughed Masha, as she began to explain everything to the stranger.

"May the saints help you!" said he, as he went his way.

When they had got the legs, arms, hands, feet, and head fixed up together, Akem began making the nose, two holes for the eyes, and was just drawing a small line for the mouth, when he suddenly, much to his surprise, felt warm breath come out of it. He took his hand away quickly, and on looking up at the two holes made for the eyes, beheld two real, beautiful blue eyes; the lips became full and rosy, and as for the nose, it was the dearest little nose ever seen.

"Good heavens! What does this mean? Is it a temptation of the Evil One?" cried Akem, crossing himself several times, while the snow child threw her arms round his neck, and kissed him as though she were alive.

"O Akem! Akem!" cried Masha, trembling with joy, "Providence has at last taken pity on us, and sent us this child to cheer us in our old age."

She was about to throw her arms around the snow child and embrace it, when, to the astonishment of both the old man and woman, the snow fell off, and left in Masha's arms a beautiful little girl.

"Oh, my little Snow Maiden! my little darling!" cried the happy Masha, as she led the lovely child into their hut. Meanwhile, Akem could not get over his wonder. He rubbed his head, and felt sorely puzzled; he did not know whether he was asleep or awake, but felt almost sure that something had gone wrong with him somewhere.

But to return to the Snow Maiden (as Masha was pleased to call her). She grew very rapidly — not only daily but hourly — into a tall, beautiful, and graceful girl; the peasants were delighted with her — Akem had come to the conclusion that it was all right — their hut was now always in constant mirth. The village girls and boys were frequent visitors to it; they played, read, and sang with the Snow Maiden, who understood it all thoroughly, and did her best to amuse all around her. She talked, laughed, and was altogether so cheerful and good natured, that everybody loved her dearly, and tried to please her in every possible way, — at the same time a better and more obedient daughter never was. She had the most lovely white skin, just like snow; her eyes were like forget-me-nots, her lips and cheeks like roses; in fact, she was the very picture of health and beauty; with her lovely golden hair hanging down her back, she looked just like a girl of seventeen, though she was only a few days old.

"Akem," said Masha, one day to her husband, "how good Providence has been to us; how Snow Maiden has brightened us, in these few days, and how wicked we were to grumble as we did."

"Yes, Masha," returned Akem, "we ought to thank Providence for all that He has done for us, and thank Him that we have mirth instead of gloom, in our little home."

Winter passed, the heavens rejoiced, the spring Sun came out, the swallows began to fly about, and the grass and trees became green once more.

The lovely Russian peasant girls gathered themselves together, and met their young cavaliers under the trees in the forest, where they danced and sang their pretty Russian songs. But the Snow Maiden was dull.

"What is the matter with you, my darling?" asked Masha; "are you ill? You are always so bright and cheerful as a rule, and now you are so dull all at once. Has any bad man thrown a spell over you?"

"No, mother mine; nothing is the matter with me, darling," the Snow Maiden replied, but still she continued to be dull, and by degrees she lost her beautiful colour, and began to droop sadly, greatly to the alarm of those around her.

The last snow had now vanished, the gardens began to bloom, the rivers and lakes rippled, the birds sang merrily; in fact all the wide world seemed happy; yet our little Snow Maiden drooped and looked sad.

She sat with her hands folded in the coolest part of the hut. She loved the cold winter, it was her best friend, but this horrid heat she hated. She was glad when it rained a little, there was no broiling Sun then. She did not mind the winter Sun, but the summer Sun was her enemy; and quite natural, too, poor thing, when she was born in the winter in the snow! At last the great summer feast arrived, the village youths and maidens came to the Snow Maiden and asked her to join them in a romp through the woods, and begged Masha to let her go with them. At first Masha refused, but the girls begged so hard that at last, on thinking it over, she consented, for she thought it might cheer Snow Maiden up.

"But," said she, "take care of her, for she is the apple of my eye, and if anything happens to her, I don't know what I shall do!"

"All right! All right! We shall take care of her, she is just as dear to us!" cried the young people, as they took Snow Maiden and ran off with her into the forest, where the girls wove themselves wreaths, while the young men gathered sticks, which they piled up high; and at sunset they set fire to them, and then they arranged themselves all in a row one after another, boys and girls, and prepared to jump over the burning heap. Our Snow Maiden was the last in the row.

"Mind," said the girls to her, " don't stay behind but jump after us."

One! Two! Three! And away they went, jumping over the flames in great delight. Suddenly they heard a piercing scream, and on looking round discovered that Snow Maiden was missing.

"Ah," cried they, laughing, "she is up to one of her tricks again, and has most likely gone and hidden herself somewhere. Come, let us go and search for her."

They all ran off in pairs in different directions, but nowhere could they find their missing companion. Their happy young faces soon turned very grave, and their joy gave place to sorrow and alarm. They met at last in the road outside the forest, and began asking each other what they had best do.

"Perhaps she has run home," said one.

This seemed a happy thought; so they ran to the hut, but no Snow Maiden was there. They looked for her all through the next day and night, and on the third, and fourth. They sought her in the village, hut after hut, and in the forest, tree after tree, bush after bush; but all in vain, nowhere could they find her. As for poor Akem and Masha, it is needless to say, that their grief was too great for words, no one could comfort them. Day after day, night after night, did poor Masha wander into the forest, calling like the cuckoo, "Oh, my little Snow Maiden! Oh, my little darling."

But there was no answer to her call, not one word from that sweet voice did Masha get in reply. Snow Maiden was not to be found, that was certain, but how had she vanished, and whither had she gone? Had the wild beasts of the forest eaten her up? or had the robber-bird carried her off to the blue sea? No, it was not the wild beasts, nor was it the robber-bird, but — as our little friend was jumping over the flames after her companions she evaporated into a thin cloud, and flew to the heights of the heavens.

Source: Edith M. S. Hodgetts, *Tales and Legends from the Land of the Tzar: Collection of Russian Stories*, 2nd edition (London: Griffith Farran and Company, 1891), pp. 46-52.

The Snow Daughter and the Fire Son
Bukovina

There was once upon a time a man and his wife, and they had no children, which was a great grief to them. One winter's day, when the Sun was shining brightly, the couple were standing outside their cottage, and the woman was looking at all the little icicles, which hung from the roof.

She sighed, and turning to her husband said, "I wish I had as many children as there are icicles hanging there."

"Nothing would please me more either," replied her husband.

Then a tiny icicle detached itself from the roof, and dropped into the woman's mouth, who swallowed it with a smile, and said, "Perhaps I shall give birth to a snow child now!"

Her husband laughed at his wife's strange idea, and they went back into the house.

But after a short time the woman gave birth to a little girl, who was as white as snow and as cold as ice. If they brought the child anywhere near the fire, it screamed loudly till they put it back into some cool place. The little maid throve wonderfully, and in a few months she could run about and speak. But she was not altogether easy to bring up, and gave her parents much trouble and anxiety, for all summer she insisted on spending in the cellar, and in the winter she would sleep outside in the snow, and the colder it was the happier she seemed to be. Her father and mother called her simply "Our Snow Daughter," and this name stuck to her all her life.

One day her parents sat by the fire, talking over the extraordinary behaviour of their daughter, who was disporting herself in the snowstorm that raged outside.

The woman sighed deeply and said, "I wish I had given birth to a Fire Son!" As she said these words, a spark from the big wood fire flew into the woman's lap, and she said with a laugh, "Now perhaps I shall give birth to a Fire Son!"

The man laughed at his wife's words, and thought it was a good joke. But he ceased to think it a joke when his wife shortly afterwards gave birth to a boy, who screamed lustily till he was put quite close to the fire, and who nearly yelled himself into a fit if the Snow Daughter came anywhere near him. The Snow Daughter herself avoided him as much as she could, and always crept into a corner as far away from him as possible.

The parents called the boy simply "Our Fire Son," a name which stuck to him all his life.

They had a great deal of trouble and worry with him too; but he throve and grew very quickly, and before he was a year old he could run about and talk. He was as red as fire, and as hot to touch, and he always sat on the hearth quite close to the fire, and complained of the cold; if his sister were in the room he almost crept into the flames, while the girl on her part always complained of the great heat if her brother were anywhere near. In summer the boy always lay out in the Sun, while the girl hid herself in the cellar: so it happened that the brother and sister came very little into contact with each other — in fact, they carefully avoided it.

Just as the girl grew up into a beautiful woman, her father and mother both died one after the other.

Then the Fire Son, who had grown up in the meantime into a fine, strong young man, said to his sister, "I am going out into the world, for what is the use of remaining on here?"

"I shall go with you," she answered, "for, except you, I have no one in the world, and I have a feeling that if we set out together we shall be lucky."

The Fire Son said, "I love you with all my heart, but at the same time I always freeze if you are near me, and you nearly die of heat if I approach you! How shall we travel about together without being odious the one to the other?"

"Don't worry about that," replied the girl, "for I've thought it all over, and have settled on a plan which will make us each able to bear with the other! See, I have had a fur cloak made for each of us, and if we put them on I shall not feel the heat so much nor you the cold."

So they put on the fur cloaks, and set out cheerfully on their way, and for the first time in their lives quite happy in each other's company.

For a long time the Fire Son and the Snow Daughter wandered through the world, and when at the beginning of winter they came to a big wood they determined to stay there till spring. The Fire Son built himself a hut where he always kept up a huge fire, while his sister with very few clothes on stayed outside night and day.

Now it happened one day that the king of the land held a hunt in this wood, and saw the Snow Daughter wandering about in the open air. He wondered very much who the beautiful girl clad in such garments could be, and he stopped and spoke to her. He soon learnt that she could not stand heat, and that her brother could not endure cold. The king was so charmed by the Snow Daughter, that he asked her to be his wife. The girl consented, and the wedding was held with much state.

The king had a huge house of ice made for his wife underground, so that even in summer it did not melt. But for his brother-in-law he had a house built with huge ovens all round it, that were kept heated all day and night. The Fire Son was delighted, but the perpetual heat in which he lived made his body so hot, that it was dangerous to go too close to him.

One day the king gave a great feast, and asked his brother-in-law among the other guests. The Fire Son did not appear till everyone had assembled, and when he did, everyone fled outside to the open air, so intense was the heat he gave forth.

Then the king was very angry and said, "If I had known what a lot of trouble you would have been, I would never have taken you into my house."

Then the Fire Son replied with a laugh, "Don't be angry, dear brother! I love heat and my sister loves cold. Come here and let me embrace you, and then I'll go home at once."

And before the king had time to reply, the Fire Son seized him in a tight embrace. The king screamed aloud in agony, and when his wife, the Snow Daughter, who had taken refuge from her brother in the next room, hurried to him, the king lay dead on the ground burnt to a cinder.

When the Snow Daughter saw this she turned on her brother and flew at him. Then a fight began, the like of which had never been seen on Earth. When the people, attracted by the noise, hurried to the spot, they saw the Snow Daughter melting into water and the Fire Son burn to a cinder.

And so ended the unhappy brother and sister.

Source: Andrew Lang, *The Yellow Fairy Book* (London: Longmans, Green, and Company, 1906), pp. 206-208.

Bukovina is a historic region now split between Romania and Bulgaria.

Yuki-Onna
Japan

In a village of Musashi Province, there lived two woodcutters: Mosaku and Minokichi. At the time of which I am speaking, Mosaku was an old man; and Minokichi, his apprentice, was a lad of eighteen years.

Every day they went together to a forest situated about five miles from their village. On the way to that forest there is a wide river to cross; and there is a ferry-boat. Several times a bridge was built where the ferry is; but the bridge was each time carried away by a flood. No common bridge can resist the current there when the river rises.

Mosaku and Minokichi were on their way home, one very cold evening, when a great snowstorm overtook them. They reached the ferry; and they found that the boatman had gone away, leaving his boat on the other side of the river. It was no day for swimming; and the woodcutters took shelter in the ferryman's hut, thinking themselves lucky to find any shelter at all.

There was no brazier in the hut, nor any place in which to make a fire: it was only a two-mat hut, with a single door, but no window. Mosaku and Minokichi fastened the door, and lay down to rest, with their straw raincoats over them. At first they did not feel very cold; and they thought that the storm would soon be over.

The old man almost immediately fell asleep; but the boy, Minokichi, lay awake a long time, listening to the awful wind, and the continual slashing of the snow against the door. The river was roaring; and the hut swayed and creaked like a junk at sea. It was a terrible storm; and the air was every moment becoming colder; and

Minokichi shivered under his rain-coat. But at last, in spite of the cold, he too fell asleep.

He was awakened by a showering of snow in his face. The door of the hut had been forced open; and, by the snow-light (yuki-akan), he saw a woman in the room, a woman all in white. She was bending above Mosaku, and blowing her breath upon him; and her breath was like a bright white smoke. Almost in the same moment she turned to Minokichi, and stooped over him. He tried to cry out, but found that he could not utter any sound. The white woman bent down over him, lower and lower, until her face almost touched him; and he saw that she was very beautiful, though her eyes made him afraid.

For a little time she continued to look at him; then she smiled, and she whispered, "I intended to treat you like the other man. But I cannot help feeling some pity for you, because you are so young. . . . You are a pretty boy, Minokichi; and I will not hurt you now. But, if you ever tell anybody -- even your own mother — about what you have seen this night, I shall know it; and then I will kill you. . . . Remember what I say!"

With these words, she turned from him, and passed through the doorway. Then he found himself able to move; and he sprang up, and looked out. But the woman was nowhere to be seen; and the snow was driving furiously into the hut. Minokichi closed the door, and secured it by fixing several billets of wood against it. He wondered if the wind had blown it open; he thought that he might have been only dreaming, and might have mistaken the gleam of the snow-light in the doorway for the figure of a white woman: but he could not be sure.

He called to Mosaku, and was frightened because the old man

did not answer. He put out his hand in the dark, and touched Mosaku's face, and found that it was ice! Mosaku was stark and dead. . . .

By dawn the storm was over; and when the ferry-man returned to his station, a little after sunrise, he found Minokichi lying senseless beside the frozen body of Mosaku. Minokichi was promptly cared for, and soon came to himself; but he remained a long time ill from the effects of the cold of that terrible night. He had been greatly frightened also by the old man's death; but he said nothing about the vision of the woman in white.

As soon as he got well again, he returned to his calling, going alone every morning to the forest, and coming back at nightfall with his bundles of wood, which his mother helped him to sell.

One evening, in the winter of the following year, as he was on his way home, he overtook a girl who happened to be travelling by the same road. She was a tall, slim girl, very good-looking; and she answered Minokichi's greeting in a voice as pleasant to the ear as the voice of a song-bird. Then he walked beside her; and they began to talk. The girl said that her name was O-Yuki [this name, signifying Snow, is not uncommon]; that she had lately lost both of her parents; and that she was going to Yedo, where she happened to have some poor relations, who might help her to find a situation as servant.

Minokichi soon felt charmed by this strange girl; and the more that he looked at her, the handsomer she appeared to be. He asked her whether she was yet betrothed; and she answered, laughingly, that she was free. Then, in her turn, she asked Minokichi whether he was married, or pledged to marry; and he told her that, although he had only a widowed mother to support, the question of an "honourable daughter-in-law" had not yet been considered, as he was very young.

. .

After these confidences, they walked on for a long while without speaking; but, as the proverb declares, Ki ga aréba, mé mo kuchi hodo ni mono wo iu: "When the wish is there, the eyes can say as much as the mouth."

By the time they reached the village, they had become very much pleased with each other; and then Minokichi asked 0-Yuki to rest awhile at his house. After some shy hesitation, she went there with him; and his mother made her welcome, and prepared a warm meal for her.

0-Yuki behaved so nicely that Minokichi's mother took a sudden fancy to her, and persuaded her to delay her journey to Yedo. And the natural end of the matter was that 0-Yuki never went to Yedo at all. She remained in the house, as an "honourable daughter-in-law."

0-Yuki proved a very good daughter-in-law. When Minokichi's mother came to die, some five years later, her last words were words of affection and praise for the wife of her son. And 0-Yuki bore Minokichi ten children, boys and girls, handsome children all of them, and very fair of skin.

The country-folk thought 0-Yuki a wonderful person, by nature different from themselves. Most of the peasant women age early; but 0-Yuki, even after having become the mother of ten children, looked as young and fresh as on the day when she had first come to the village.

One night, after the children had gone to sleep, 0-Yuki was sewing by the light of a paper lamp; and Minokichi, watching her, said, "To see you sewing there, with the light on your face, makes me think of a strange thing that happened when I was a lad of eighteen. I then saw somebody as beautiful and white as you are now; indeed, she was very like you." . . .

Without lifting her eyes from her work, 0-Yuki responded, "Tell me about her. . . . Where did you see her?"

Then Minokichi told her about the terrible night in the ferryman's hut, and about the White Woman that had stooped above him, smiling and whispering, and about the silent death of old Mosaku.

And he said, "Asleep or awake, that was the only time that I saw a being as beautiful as you. Of course, she was not a human being; and I was afraid of her, very much afraid; but she was so white! . . . Indeed, I have never been sure whether it was a dream that I saw, or the Woman of the Snow." . . .

0-Yuki flung down her sewing, and arose, and bowed above Minokichi where he sat, and shrieked into his face, "It was I — I — I! 0-Yuki it was! And I told you then that I would kill you if you ever said one word about it! . . . But for those children asleep there, I would kill you this moment! And now you had better take very, very good care of them; for if ever they have reason to complain of you, I will treat you as you deserve!" . . .

Even as she screamed, her voice became thin, like a crying of wind; then she melted into a bright white mist that spired to the roof-beams, and shuddered away through the smoke-hole. . . . Never again was she seen.

Source: Lafcadio Hearn, Kwaidan: *Stories and Studies of Strange Things,* Leipzig: Bernhard Tauchnitz, (1907), pp. 123-32.

Where "The Two Magicians" Come From

"The Two Magicians" first appears in print in 1828 in two sources, Peter Buchan's *Ancient Ballads and Songs of the North of Scotland* and John Wilson's *Noctes Ambrosianae* #40. It was later published as number 44 of Francis James Child's *English and Scottish Popular Ballads*, and it is this version that is presented below.

The ballad tells the tale of a blacksmith. He threatens to take the virginity of a lady, but she vows to keep herself a maiden. A transformation chase ensues, differing in several variants, but containing such things as she becomes a hare, and he catches her as greyhound, she became a duck and he became either a water dog or a drake.

Francis James Child (1825 – 1896) was an American scholar, educator, and folklorist, best known today for his collection of folk songs known as the Child Ballads. These were published in five volumes between 1882 and 1898.

Child believed "The Two Magicians" to be derived from one of two fairy tale forms. In the first, a young man and woman flee an enemy by taking on new forms. This type is Aarne-Thompson type 313, the girl helps the hero flee; instances of it include "Jean, the Soldier, and Eulalie, the Devil's Daughter", "The Grateful Prince", "Foundling-Bird", and "The Two Kings' Children". In the second, a young man, studying with a sorcerer, flees his master by taking on new forms, which his master counters by equivalent forms. This is

Aarne-Thompson type 325, the magician and his pupil; instances include "The Thief and His Master", "Master and Pupil", and "Maestro Lattantio and His Apprentice Dionigi". There is also the Scandinavian tale of "Farmer Weathersky", in which Weathersky – in reality the Devil – is out-shifted by a young hero named, in English translation, Jack (see McCormick & Kennedy White, 2010, p.1144)

Another suggestion that has been made is the ballad has links with the Welsh tale of the birth of Taliesin. Gwion, servant of Ceridwen, accidentally drinks three drops of magic potion from her Cauldron of Inspiration. The furious Ceridwen chases after him, and they both shape-shift as he tries to escape her. Finally Gwion turns himself into a grain of corn. Ceridwen turns into a hen and eats him, and nine months later gives birth to Taliesin. However, as it will be shown, the likelihood is that the origins of "The Two Magicians" can be traced back even further into the past.

One of the attributes often credited to shamans, as well as to witches and other kinds of magical practitioner, is the ability to shape-shift from human into animal shape. Sometimes this change is a literal one, human flesh transformed into animal flesh or covered over by animal skin; in other accounts, the soul leaves the shaman's unconscious body to enter into the body of an animal, fish or bird. And it is not only shamans who have such powers according to tales from around the globe. Shape shifting is part of a mythic and story-telling tradition stretching back over thousands of years. The Gods of various mythologies are credited with this ability, as are the heroes of the great epic sagas.

In Nordic myth, Odin could change his shape into any beast or bird; in Greek myth, Zeus often assumed animal shape in his relentless pursuit of young women. Cernunnos, the lord of animals in Celtic mythology, wore the shape of a stag, and also the shape of a man with a heavy rack of horns. In the *Odyssey*, Homer tells the tale of Proteus—a famous soothsayer who would not give away his knowledge unless forced to do so. Menelaus came upon him while he slept, and held on to him tightly as he shape-shifted into a lion, a snake, a leopard, a bear, etc. Defeated, Proteus returned to his own shape and Menelaus won the answers to his questions (Berman, 2007, pp.134-135).

There are stories of shape-shifting in our folklore too. The Great Selkie of Sule Skerry described in Scottish ballads, is a man upon dry land, a selkie [seal] in the sea, and he leaves a human maid pregnant with his child. And Irish legends tell of men who marry seal or otter women and then hide their animal skins from them to prevent them from returning to the water. Generally these women bear several sons, but pine away for their true home. If they manage to find the skin, they then return to the sea with barely a thought for the ones left behind.

Additionally, there is strong, though not conclusive, archaeological evidence to indicate that what we call shamanism was once practised in this land:

[In Upton Lovell in Wiltshire there is a round barrow covering] an adult male skeleton with rows of thin, perforated bones about his neck, thighs and feet. They had almost certainly hung in fringes from his clothes. With him were fine stone axe-heads, boars' tusks, white flints and pebbles of a stone not found in the area. A similar mound at Youlgreave, Derbyshire, held a man with the teeth of a dog and a horse under his head and a round bronze amulet on his chest. With him were an ace, quartz pebbles and a piece of porphyry. The ashes of another burial from a lost barrow near Stonehenge were mixed with four stained rectangular bronze tablets, one plain and the others incised with a cross or a star or a lozenge (Bronze Age Tarot cards?). All these suggest the presence not so much of a priesthood as of shamans or medicine people, familiar in the tribal peoples of the modern world (Hutton, 1993, p.109).

This leads us to believe that there could well be a shamanic past behind Beowulf and other Old English poems and early poetry could well be an art form rooted in tribal tradition that therefore retains traces of native beliefs. "Too many reflexes occur in the literature for us to ignore the influential role shamanism played in Anglo-Saxon prehistory" (Glosecki, 1989, p.3), and how it went on to influence later poetry / ballads too. It is highly likely, for example, that "descriptions of Sabbath experiences and familiar-encounters found in early modern European witch trials were expressions of popular experiential traditions rooted in pre-Christian shamanistic beliefs and practices" (Wilby, 2005, p.5). In this article, the shamanic themes to be found in "The Two Magicians", Child Ballad 44, will be explored.

The term 'shaman' is a controversial one. Initially employed by early anthropologists to refer to a specific category of magical practitioners from Siberia, the term is now widely used to denote similar practitioners from a variety of cultures around the world. This application of an originally culture-specific term to a more general usage has caused problems with regard to definition, with disagreements among scholars over whether certain features, such as soul flight or possession, or certain types of altered states of consciousness, should or should not be listed among the core characteristics of shamanism (Wilby, 2011, p.252).

As a result, there are as many definitions of shamanism as there are books written on the subject. Here is my version:

A shaman is someone who performs an ecstatic (in a trance state), imitative, or demonstrative ritual of a séance (or a combination of all three), at will (in other words, whenever he or she chooses to do so), in which by means of a shamanic journey, aid is sought from beings in (what are considered to be) other realities generally for healing purposes or for divination–both for individuals and / or the community.

A shamanic journey is one that generally takes place in a trance state to the sound of a drumbeat, through dancing, or by ingesting psychoactive drugs, in which aid is sought from beings in (what are considered to be) other realities generally for healing purposes or for divination–both for individuals and / or the community.

As for shamanic ballads, they are based on or inspired by shamanic journeys, and contain a number of the elements typical of such journeys. They consist of ballad-types where a being with supernatural powers plays an integral and necessary part in the central ballad action, and these "beings with supernatural powers fall into four classes: supernatural beings; supernatural ex-mortals; mortals with supernatural powers; and creatures with supernatural powers" (Harris, 1991, p.64).

In "The Two Magicians", both the blacksmith and the lady can perhaps best be described as mortals with supernatural powers or, in other words, shamanic practitioners. As is the case with the shaman of a community, the work of the blacksmith involves the transformation of forms too, and there is traditionally a strong association between the two.

What can be concluded from this is that what initially appears to be little more than a tale of seduction, could well have originally been based upon a shape-shifting contest.

Further accounts of such contests can be found in joiks. A joik is a traditional Sami form of song, mainly chanted a cappella, and often dedicated to a human being, an animal, or a landscape as a personal signature. A number of these were about "the duels" that used to take place between the noaidis (shamans), like the joik text dedicated to the noaidi Gargias:

[It is] a story about a contest between two infamous shamans in two adjoining areas of Samiland. In the initial situation all of the wild game has disappeared from Gargias' district, and through the trance he has been placed in at the very beginning of the yoik, he knows that the reason for the famine now threatening his people is due to sorcery from the neighbouring siida's or neighbouring area's noaidi Doragas. Doragas, you see, had led all the wild game in the forests and all the fish in the rivers and lakes over to the neighbouring district. With the help of his *sieidi* – sacrificial stone or god – Gargias however manages to yoik the game and fish back again. Doragas doesn't put up with this debasement; he kills Gargias and throws him out into the river. But Gargias is still not dead; he transforms himself into a little object that a pike swallows.

Gargias is in the pike stomach an entire year until Doragas understands that Gargias is still alive and hiding in a pike. So Doragas puts out a net to catch the pike, but Gargias escapes. For three years he is left alone by Doragas until one beautiful day on the way home to the turf hut after a hunting trip he is again killed. This time Doragas puts him in a chest and lets him lie there for another three years, but during the funeral Gargias revives again and slips out of the chest. He calls his son, presumably to demonstrate before the crowd of people at the cemetery what a powerful shaman he really is as well as to disavow Doragas even more. However, his son has also learned the shamanistic arts during his father's absence and comes flying in the shape of a wood grouse. This emphasis on the son's knowledge at a point in time when the father is really supposed to shine insults Gargias and makes him so angry that the whole thing ends in a fateful clash between father and son with the result that the son flies off and leaves his father behind humbled and sorrowful. The unfortunate consequence for Gargias' people from this internal struggle was of course that their noaidi lost power and respect and that the riches of the forests and lakes once again to another group. (Taken from 'When the Thieves Became Masters in the Land of the Shamans' by Harald Gaski and translated by John Weinstock www.utexas.edu/courses/sami/diehtu/giella/music/tyven.htm [accessed 26/12/2011]).

And not only in former times, but even today on Neo-shamanic workshops, pair work activities that involve trainees searching for each other in non-ordinary reality are incorporated into workshops in order to develop the apprentices' skills.

The Two Magicians

44.1   THE lady stands in her bower door,
As straight as willow wand;
The blacksmith stood a little forebye,
Wi hammer in his hand.

44.2   'Weel may ye dress ye, lady fair,
Into your robes o red;
Before the morn at this same time,
I'll gain your maidenhead.'

44.3   'Awa, awa, ye coal-black smith,
        Woud ye do me the wrang
        To think to gain my maidenhead,
        That I hae kept sae lang!'

44.4   Then she has hadden up her hand,
        And she sware by the mold,
        'I wudna be a blacksmith's wife
        For the full o a chest o gold.

44.5   'I'd rather I were dead and gone,
        And my body laid in grave,
        Ere a rusty stock o coal-black smith
        My maidenhead shoud have.'

44.6   But he has hadden up his hand,
        And he sware by the mass,
        'I'll cause ye be my light leman
        For the hauf o that and less.'

44.6b   O bide, lady, bide,
        And aye he bade her bide;
        The rusty smith your leman shall be,
        For a' your muckle pride.

44.7   Then she became a turtle dow,
        To fly up in the air,
        And he became another dow,
        And they flew pair and pair.

44.7b   O bide, lady, bide, 'C..

44.8   She turnd hersell into an eel,
         To swim into yon burn,
         And he became a speckled trout,
         To gie the eel a turn.

44.8b   O bide, lady, bide, 'C..

44.9   Then she became a duck, a duck,
         To puddle in a peel,
         And he became a rose-kaimd drake,
         To gie the duck a dreel.

44.9b   O bide, lady, bide, 'C..

44.10   She turnd hersell into a hare,
         To rin upon yon hill,
         And he became a gude grey-hound,
         And boldly he did fill.

44.10b   O bide, lady, bide, 'C..

44.11   Then she became a gay grey mare,
         And stood in yonder slack,
         And he became a gilt saddle,
         And sat upon her back.

44.11b   Was she wae, he held her sae,

> And still he bade her bide;
> The rusty smith her leman was,
> For a' her muckle pride.

44.12   Then she became a het girdle,
> And he became a cake,
> And a' the ways she turnd hersell,
> The blacksmith was her make.

44.12b Was she wae, etc.

44.13   She turnd hersell into a ship,
> To sail out ower the flood;
> He ca'ed a nail intill her tail,
> And syne the ship she stood.

44.13b Was she wae, etc.

44.14   Then she became a silken plaid,
> And stretchd upon a bed,
> And he became a green covering,
> And gaind her maidenhead.

44.14b Was she wae, etc.

Writing or talking about shamanism has always been problematic as "the subject area resists 'objective' analysis and is sufficiently beyond mainstream research to foil ...writing [or talking] about it in

SHAPE-SHIFTERS AND THEIR STORIES *123*

a conventional academic way" (Wallis, 2003, p.13). Shamans have their own ways of describing trance experience.

Outsiders might call them 'metaphors', but to shamans these metaphors, such as 'death', are real, lived experiences ... Metaphor is a problematic term extracted from Western literary discourse which does not do justice to non-Western, non-literary shamanic experiences. In recognizing this limitation, metaphor may remain a useful term for explaining alien shamanic experiences in terms understandable to Westerners (Wallis, 2003, p.116).

Perhaps this is why the accounts of memorable shamanic journeys were often turned into folk-tales or ballads, as it was the only way to make them both understandable and acceptable to people not familiar with the landscapes to be found and experiences to be had in such worlds.

References

Berman, M. (2007) *The Nature of Shamanism and the Shamanic Story*, Newcastle: Cambridge Scholars Publishing.

Child, F. J. *The English and Scottish Popular Ballads*. Boston, New York, Houghton, Mifflin and Company [1886-98]. Ballads originally transcribed by Cathy Lynn Preston. HTML Formatting at sacred-texts.com. This text is in the public domain.

Glosecki, S.O. (1989) *Shamanism and Old English Poetry*, New York: Garland Publishing Inc.

Harris, J. (1991) *The Ballad and Oral Literature*, Harvard University Press.

Hutton, R. (1993) *The Pagan Religions of the Ancient British Isles: Their Nature and Legacy*, Oxford: Blackwell Publishing.

McCormick, C. T., & Kennedy White, K. (2010) *Folklore: An*

Encyclopedia of Beliefs, Customs, Tales, Music, and Art, ABC-Clio Inc. 2nd edition.

Wallis, Robert J. (2003) *Shamans/Neo-Shamans: Ecstasy, Alternative Archaeologies and Contemporary Pagans*, London: Routledge.

Wilby, E. (2005) *Cunning Folk and Familiar Spirits: Shamanistic Visionary Traditions in Early Modern British Witchcraft and Magic*, Brighton: Sussex Academic Press.

The Golem

All life is connected and there is life in everything, even a lump of clay, with the help of a little bit of magic. In the legend of the Golem, persecuted Jews create an artificial monster to protect themselves from their enemies. It is a tale that might well have prompted Mary Shelley to write her famous novel about Dr. Frankenstein and his man-like creation.

The Golem is perhaps the best-known mythical creature in Jewish literature. It has been the source for numerous stories, plays and artistic renditions, and its origin is based on a legend about Rabbi Judah Loew, who lived in Prague during the 16th century. According to the legend, Rabbi Loew created the Golem to protect the Jewish people against their oppressors.

At one time, images of the Golem could be found on European architecture as protective emblems against evil forces, but perhaps the main reason why the legend lives on is the generations of visitors who return to Prague each year in search of the Golem's mythical beginnings.

The Golem

In the town of Worms, in Germany, there once lived a pious man by the name of Bezalel to whom a son was born on the first night of Passover. This happened in the year 5273 after the creation of the world [1579 common era], at a time when the Jews all over Europe were suffering from cruel persecutions.

The Jews, their enemies pretended, used the blood of Christian children in the preparation of their unleavened bread for Passover; but the arrival of the son of Rabbi Bezalel soon proved to be the occasion of frustrating the evil intentions of two miscreants who sought to show to Christendom that the Jews were actually guilty of ritual murder.

In the night, when the wife of Rabbi Bezalel was seized with labour pains, the servants who had rushed out of the house in search of a midwife luckily prevented two men, who were just going to throw a sack containing the body of a dead child into the Jew-street, with a view to proving the murderous practice of the Jews, from carrying out their evil intention. Rabbi Bezalel then prophesied that his newborn son was destined to bring consolation to Israel and to save his people from such accusations.

"The name of my son in Israel," said Rabbi Bezalel "shall be Judah Arya, even as the Patriarch Jacob said when he blessed his children: 'Judah is a lion's whelp; from the prey, my son, thou art gone up.'" (Genesis 49:9)

Rabbi Bezalel's son grew up and increased in strength and knowledge; he became a great scholar, well versed in the Holy Law, but also a master of all branches of knowledge and familiar with many foreign languages. In time he was elected Rabbi of Posen [in Poland], but later received a call to the city of Prague, where he was appointed chief judge of the Jewish community.

All his thoughts and actions were devoted to the welfare of his suffering people and his great aim in life was to clear Israel of the monstrous accusation of ritual murder which, like a sword of Damocles, was perpetually suspended over the head of the unhappy race. Fervently did the rabbi pray to Heaven to teach him in a vision how he could best bring to naught the false accusations of the miscreant priests who were spreading the cruel rumours.

And one night he heard a mysterious voice calling to him, "Make a human image of clay and that is how you will succeed in frustrating the evil intentions of the enemies of Israel."

On the following morning the master called his son-in-law and his favourite pupil and acquainted them with the instruction he had received from Heaven. He also asked the two to help him in the work he was about to undertake.

"Four elements," he said, "are required for the creation of the Golem or homunculus, namely, earth, water, fire and air."

"I myself," thought the holy man, "possess the power of the wind; my son-in-law embodies fire, while my favourite pupil is the symbol of water, and between the three of us we are bound to succeed in our work." He urged on his companions the necessity of great secrecy and asked them to spend seven days in preparing for the work.

On the twentieth day of the month of Adar, in the year five thousand three hundred and forty after the creation of the world, in the fourth hour after midnight, the three men betook themselves to a river on the outskirts of the city on the banks of which they found a loam pit. Here they kneaded the soft clay and fashioned the figure of a man three ells high. They fashioned the features, hands and feet, and then placed the figure of clay on its back upon the ground.

The three learned men then stood at the feet of the image which they had created and the rabbi commanded his son-in-law to walk round the figure seven times, while reciting a cabalistic formula he had himself composed. And as soon as the son-in-law had completed the seven rounds and recited the formula, the figure of clay grew red like a gleaming coal. The rabbi then commanded his pupil to perform the same action, namely, walk round the lifeless figure seven times while reciting another formula. The effect of the performance was this time an abatement of the heat. The figure grew moist and vapours emanated from it, while nails sprouted on the tips of its fingers and its head was suddenly covered with hair. The face of the figure of clay looked like that of a man of about thirty.

At last the rabbi himself walked seven times round the figure, and the three men recited the following sentence from the history of creation in Genesis: "And the Lord God formed man of the dust of the ground, and breathed into his nostrils the breath of life; and man became a living soul." (Genesis 2:7)

As soon as the three pious men had spoken these words, the eyes of the Golem opened and he gazed upon the rabbi and his pupils with eyes full of wonder. At this point Rabbi Loew spoke aloud to the man of clay and commanded him to rise from the ground. The Golem at once obeyed and stood erect on his feet. The three men then dressed the figure in the clothes they had brought with them, clothes worn by the beadles of the synagogues, and put shoes on his feet.

And the rabbi once more addressed the newly fashioned image of clay and this is what he said: "Know you, clod of clay, that we have fashioned you from the dust of the earth that you may protect the people of Israel against its enemies and shelter it from the misery and suffering to which our nation is subjected. Your name shall be Joseph, and you shall dwell in my courtroom and perform the work of a servant. You shall obey my commands and do all that I may require of you, go through fire, jump into water or throw yourself down from a high tower."

The Golem only nodded his head as if to give his consent to the words spoken by the rabbi. His conduct was in every respect that of a human being; he could hear and understand all that was said to him, but he lacked the power of speech. And so it happened on that memorable night that while only three men had left the house of the rabbi, four returned home in the sixth hour after midnight.

The rabbi kept the matter secret, informing his household that on his way in the morning to the ritual bathing establishment he had met a beggar, and, finding him honest and innocent, had brought him home. He had the intention of engaging him as a servant to attend to the work in his schoolroom, but he forbade his household to make the man perform any other domestic work.

And from then on the Golem remained in a corner of the schoolroom, his head upon his two hands, sitting motionless. He gave the impression of a creature bereft of reason, neither understanding nor taking any notice of what was happening around him. Rabbi Loew said of him that neither fire nor water had the power to harm him, nor could any sword wound him. He had called the man of clay Joseph, in memory of Joseph Sheda mentioned in the Talmud who is said to have been half human and half spirit, and who had served the rabbis and frequently saved them from great trouble.

Rabbi Loew, the miracle worker, availed himself of the services of the Golem only on occasions when it was a question of defending his people against the blood accusations from which the Jews of Prague had to suffer greatly in those days.

Golem street

Whenever the miracle-working Rabbi Loew sent out the Golem and was anxious that he should not be seen, he used to suspend on his neck an amulet written on the skin of a hart, a talisman which rendered the man of clay invisible, while he himself was able to see everything. During the week preceding the feast of Passover the Golem wandered about in the streets of the city stopping everybody who happened to be carrying some burden on his back. It frequently occurred that the bundle contained a dead child which the miscreant intended to deposit in the Jew-street; the Golem at once tied up the man and the body with a rope which he carried in his pocket, and, leading the mischief maker to the town hall, handed him over to the authorities. The Golem's power was quite supernatural and he performed many good deeds.

A day came when a law was finally introduced declaring the blood accusation to be groundless, and the Jews breathed a sigh of relief when all further persecutions on account of alleged ritual murder were forbidden. Rabbi Loew now decided to take away the breath of life from the Golem, the figure of clay which his hands had once fashioned. He placed Joseph upon a bed and commanded his disciples once more to walk round the Golem seven times and repeat the words they had spoken when the figure was created, but this time in reverse order. When the seventh round was finished, the Golem was once more a lifeless piece of clay. They took off his clothes, and wrapping him in two old praying shawls, hid the clod of clay under a heap of old books in the rabbi's garret.

Rabbi Loew afterwards related many incidents connected with the creation of the Golem. When he was on the point of blowing the breath of life into the nostrils of the figure of clay he had created, two spirits had appeared to him; that of Joseph the demon and that of Jonathan the demon. He chose the former, the spirit of Joseph, because he had already revealed himself as the protector of the rabbis of the Talmud, but he could not endow the figure of clay with the power of speech because the living spirit inhabiting the Golem was only a sort of animal vitality and not a soul. He possessed only small powers of discernment, being unable to grasp anything belonging to the domain of real intelligence and higher wisdom.

And yet, although the Golem was not possessed of a soul, one could not fail to notice that on the Sabbath there was something peculiar in his bearing, for his face bore a friendlier and more amiable expression than it did on weekdays. It was afterwards related that every Friday Rabbi Loew used to remove the tablet on which he had written the Ineffable Name from under the Golem's tongue, as he was afraid lest the Sabbath should make the Golem immortal and men might be induced to worship him as an idol. The Golem had no inclinations, either good or bad. Whatever action he performed he did under compulsion and out of fear lest he should be turned again into dust and reduced to naught once more. Whatever was situated within ten ells above the ground or under it he could reach easily and nothing would stop him in the execution of anything that he had undertaken.

Source: Angelo S. Rappoport, *The Folklore of the Jews* (London: Soncino Press, 1937), pp. 195-203. No copyright notice.

The fact that the Golem had to be circled seven times should come as no surprise as it is a number that features prominently in a number of different traditions. The Heptad, a group or series

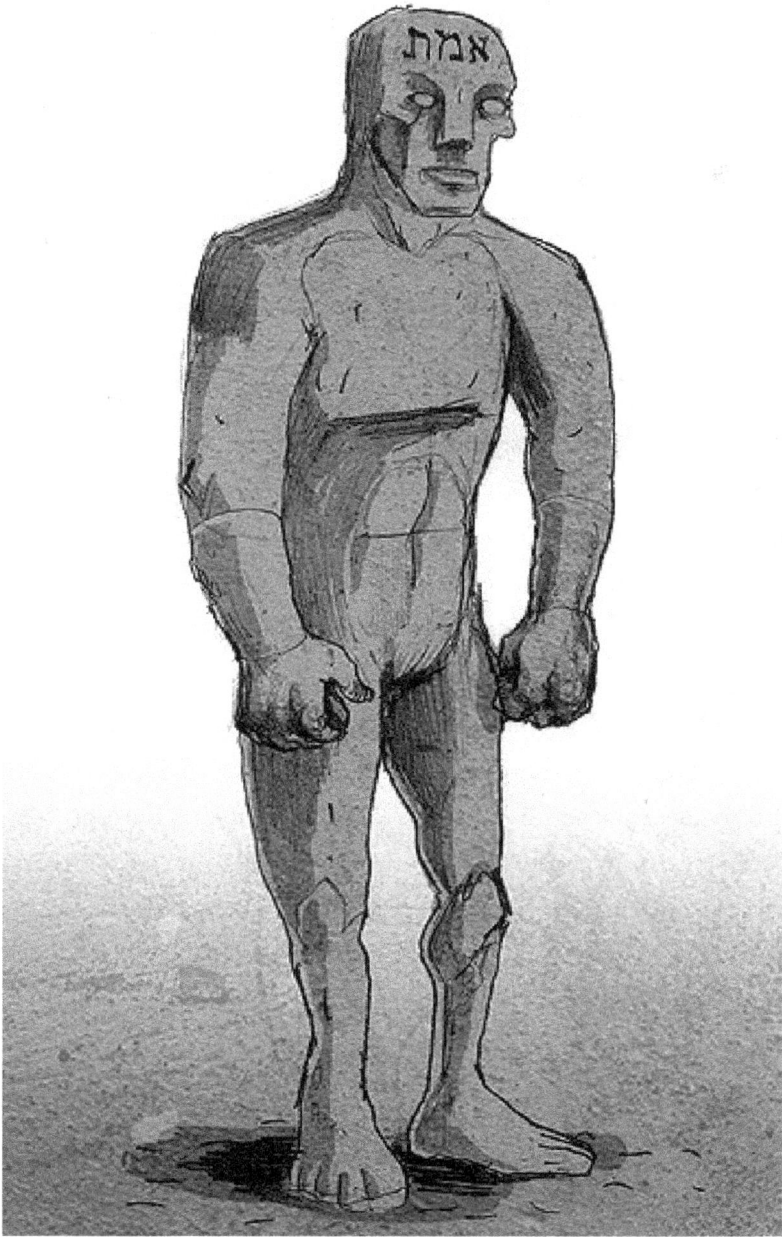

Golem by Philippe Semeria

consisting of seven items, has long been of significance for all sorts of reasons. First of all, let us consider the human body:—

The body has seven obvious parts, the head, chest, abdomen, two legs and two arms. There are seven internal organs, stomach, liver, heart, lungs, spleen and two kidneys. The ruling part, the head, has seven parts for external use, two eyes, two ears, two nostrils and a mouth. There are seven inflections of the voice, the acute, grave, circumflex, rough, smooth, the long and the short sounds. The hand makes seven motions; up and down, to the right and left, before and behind, and circular. There are seven evacuations;tears from the eyes, mucus of the nostrils, the saliva, the semen, two excretions and the perspiration. (We could also add that it is in the seventh month the human offspring becomes viable and that menstruation tends to occur in series of four times seven days).

Seven is a mystic or sacred number in many different traditions. Among the Babylonians and Egyptians, there were believed to be seven planets, and the alchemists recognized seven planets too. In the Old Testament there are seven days in creation, and for the Hebrews every seventh year was Sabbatical too. There are seven virtues, seven sins, seven ages in the life of man, seven wonders of the world, and the number seven repeatedly occurs in the Apocalypse as well. The Muslims talk of there being seven heavens, with the seventh being formed of divine light that is beyond the power of words to describe, and the Kabbalists also believe there are seven heavens–each arising above the other, with the seventh being the abode of God (Berman, 2008, p.122).

In the world of the shaman, the structure of the whole cosmos is frequently symbolized by the number seven too, "made up of the four directions, the centre, the zenith in heaven, and the nadir in the

Underworld. The essential axes of this structure are the four cardinal points and a central vertical axis passing through their point of intersection that connects the Upper World, the Middle World and the Lower World" (Berman, 2007, p.45).

As to the sacredness of the number 7, among the Hebrews oaths were confirmed by seven witnesses or by seven victims offered in sacrifice (cf. the covenant between Abraham and Abimelech with seven lambs, Genesis, chap. xxi. vv. 28, 21–28). The Persian Sun God, Mithras, had the number 7 sacred to him too.

The highest beings in Zoroastrianism, the Amshaspands, are also seven in number; Ormuzd, source of life; Bahman, the king of this world; Ardibehest, fire producer; Shahrivar, the former of metals; Spandarmat, queen of the earth (the Gnostic Sophia); Khordad, the ruler of times and seasons; and Amerdad, ruling over the vegetable world.

Sanskrit lore has very frequent reference to the number seven too:— Sapta Rishi, seven sages; Sapta Kula, 7 castes; Sapta Loka, seven worlds; Sapta Para, 7 cities; Sapta Dwipa, seven holy islands; Sapta Arania, 7 deserts; Sapta Parna, 7 human principles; Sapta Samudra, seven holy seas; Sapta Vruksha, 7 holy trees.

The Assyrian Tablets also teem with groups of sevens:— 7 gods of sky; 7 gods of earth; 7 gods of fiery spheres: seven gods maleficent; seven phantoms; spirits of seven heavens; spirits of seven earths.

The Moon passes through stages of 7 days in increase, full, decrease, and renewal, and in addition to the seven stars in the head of Taurus called the Pleiades, there are the seven stars which guided the sailors.

The Kabbalists describe Seven classes of Angels: Ishim, Arelim, Chashmalim, Melakim, Auphanim, Seraphim and Kerubim. The

Judaic Hell was given seven names by the Kabbalists too; Sheol, Abaddon, Tihahion, Bar Shacheth, Tzelmuth, Shaari Muth, and Gehinnom.

Other heptads can be added to those above too:— The seven prophetesses in the Old Testament are Sarah, Miriam, Deborah, Hannah, Abigail, Huldah and Esther; The 7 Catholic Deadly Sins are Pride, covetousness, lust, anger, gluttony, envy and sloth; The 7 Gifts of the Holy Spirit (Isaiah xi. v. 2) are Wisdom, Understanding, Counsel, Fortitude, Knowledge, Piety and Fear of the Lord; The 7 Champions of Christendom were St. George for England, St. Denis of France, St. James of Spain, St. Andrew of Scotland, St. David of Wales, St. Patrick of Ireland, and St. Antonio of Italy.

We can also add the historic city of Rome to the list, which was built upon Seven Hills; the Palatine, Cœlian, Aventine, Viminal, Quirinal, Esquiline, and the Capitol (adapted from 'The Heptad'. In Westcott, 1911, pp. 72-84).

Last but not least, mention should be made of what have been described as the seven basic plots (see Booker, 2004), and the suggestion that all the stories that have ever been written are based on these. The seven basic plot types Christopher Booker identifies are Overcoming The Monster, Rags to Riches, The Quest, Voyage and Return, Comedy, Tragedy, and Rebirth. And "The Golem" is perhaps best described as overcoming the monster of persecution by creating a monster.

Legends, unlike folk-tales, were once believed to be true and, who knows, there might well have once been a person with Golem-like powers the people would have turned to for help. And even if there had not been such a figure, there would clearly have been a need to create one, for without hope there is nothing to keep us going when times get hard.

References

Berman, M. (2007) *The Nature of Shamanism and the Shamanic Story*, Newcastle: Cambridge Scholars Publishing.

Berman, M. (2008) *Divination and the Shamanic Story*, Newcastle: Cambridge Scholars Publishing.

Booker, C. (2004) *The Seven Basic Plots*, London: Continuum Books.

Westcott, W.W. (1911) (3rd Edition) *Numbers, Their Occult Power and Mystic Virtues*, London, Benares: Theosophical Pub. Society. Scanned, proofed and formatted at sacred-texts.com, August 2009, by John Bruno Hare. This text is in the public domain in the US because it was published prior to 1923.

Whenever something makes my blood boil, the failure of public services for example, I visualise the return of the Golem to help sort things out and it makes me feel a whole lot better. Perhaps it can work for you too, and it is something you might like to consider the next time you feel you are about to explode with rage. You might even like to place a representation of the Golem under your pillow each night before you sleep to fight all your battles for you.

Worry dolls (muñecas quitapenas), which can be used to serve a similar purpose to that of the Golem placed under the pillow, are very small and colourful dolls traditionally made in Guatemala. A person (usually a child) who cannot sleep due to worrying can express their worries to a doll and place it under their pillow before going to sleep. Some medical centers use them in conjunction with treatment for disease in children. According to folklore, the doll is thought to

The Old-New Synagogue in Prague
and the home of the Golem

worry in the person's place, thereby permitting the person to sleep peacefully. The person will wake up without their worries, which have been taken away by the dolls during the night. Parents may then remove the doll during the night, reinforcing the child's belief that the worry is gone.

Maharal statue, Prague

Tree and Mountain Spirits from Japan: An Animistic view of the World

A nimism (from Latin anima "soul, life") refers to the belief that non-human entities are spiritual beings, or at least embody some kind of life-principle. It is based on the principle that there is in fact no separation between the spiritual and physical (or material) world, and souls or spirits exist, not only in humans, but also in all other animals, plants, rocks, geographic features such as mountains or rivers, or other entities of the natural environment. Animism may further attribute souls to abstract concepts such as words, true names, or metaphors in mythology. Examples of animism can be found in Shinto, the indigenous spirituality of Japan, which is where the three stories in this Chapter come from.

The word Shinto ("Way of the Gods") was adopted from the written Chinese (神道), pinyin: shén dào), combining two kanji: "shin" (神), meaning "spirit" or kami; and "tô" (道), meaning a philosophical path or study (from the Chinese word dào). Kami are defined in English as "spirits", "essences" or "deities" that are associated with many understood formats; in some cases being human-like, in others being animistic, and others being associated with more abstract "natural" forces in the world (mountains, rivers, lightning, wind, waves, trees, rocks). Kami and people are not separate; they exist within the same world and share its interrelated complexity.

In the stories that follow, we find a tree spirit that shape-shifts into a woman, the God of Love who shape-shifts into a man and the Goddess of the great Mount Fuji who shape-shifts into a woman.

Willow Wife

In a certain Japanese village there grew a great willow tree. For many generations the people

loved it. In the summer it was a resting place, a place where the villagers might meet after the work and heat of the day were over, and there talk till the Moonlight streamed through the branches. In winter it was like a great half-opened umbrella covered with sparkling snow.

Heitaro, a young farmer, lived quite near this tree, and the imposing willow was very important to him. It was almost the first object he saw when he woke up each day, and when he returned from work in the fields he looked out eagerly for its familiar form. Sometimes he would kneel down and pray beneath its branches. One day an old man of the village came to Heitaro and explained to him that the villagers were anxious to build a bridge over the river, and that they wanted the tree for timber.

"For timber?" said Heitaro, hiding his face in his hands. "My dear willow tree for a bridge?

Never, never, old man!" When Heitaro had somewhat recovered himself, he offered to give the old man some of his own trees instead if he and the villagers would spare the ancient willow.

The old man readily accepted this offer, and the willow tree continued to stand in the village as it had stood for so many years.

One night while Heitaro sat under the great willow he suddenly saw a beautiful woman standing close beside him, looking at him shyly, as if she wanted to speak.

"Honourable lady," he said, "I'll go home now. I can see you're waiting for someone. Heitaro is not without kindness towards those who love."

"He won't come now," said the woman, smiling.

"Can he have grown cold? How terrible it is when a false love comes and leaves ashes and a grave behind!"

"He hasn't grown cold, dear lord."

"And yet he doesn't come! What strange mystery is this?"

"He has come! His heart's always been here, here under this willow tree." And with a radiant

smile the woman disappeared.

Night after night they met under the old willow tree. The woman's shyness had entirely disappeared, and it seemed that she could not hear too much from Heitaro's lips in praise of the willow where they sat.

One night he said to her, "Little one, will you be my wife — you who seem to come from the very tree itself?"

"Yes," said the woman. "Call me Higo ("Willow") and, if you love me, ask no questions. I've got no father or mother, and someday perhaps you'll understand."

Heitaro and Higo got married. In due time they were blessed with a child whom they called

Chiyodo, and they were the happiest people in all Japan.

One day great news came to the village. The villagers were full

of it, and it was not long before it reached Heitaro's ears. The ex-Emperor Toba wished to build a temple to Kwannon [The Goddess of Mercy] in Kyoto, and those in authority sent far and wide for timber. The villagers decided that they must contribute towards the building by presenting their great willow tree. Heitaro's promise of other trees was ineffectual this time because neither he nor anyone else could give such a large and handsome tree as the great willow.

Heitaro went home and told his wife the dreadful news. "Before I married you I couldn't have borne it," he said. "But having you, little one, perhaps I'll get over it someday."

That night Heitaro was woken up by a piercing cry.

"Heitaro," said his wife, "it grows dark! The room is full of whispers. Are you there, Heitaro?

Listen! They're cutting down the willow tree. Look how its shadow trembles in the Moonlight. I'm the soul of the willow tree. The villagers are killing me. They're tearing me to pieces! The pain, the pain!

"My Willow Wife! My Willow Wife!" sobbed Heitaro.

"Husband," said Higo, very faintly, pressing her wet, agonized face close to his, "I'm going now. But a love like ours can never be cut down, however fierce the blows, and I'll be waiting for you and Chiyodo on the other side. My hair's falling through the sky! My body's breaking!"

There was a loud crash outside. The great willow tree lay cut down on the ground. Heitaro

looked round for the one he loved more than anything else in the world. Willow Wife had gone!

This traditional Japanese tale is an adaptation of a story in *Myths and Legends of Japan* by F. Hadland Davis, published by G. G. Harrap and Company in 1913.

The Holy Cherry Tree of Musubi-no-kami Temple

IN the province of Mimasaka is a small town called Kagami, and in

the temple grounds is a shrine which has been there for some hundreds of years, and is dedicated to Musubi-no-Kami, the God of Love. Near by once stood a magnificent old cherry tree which was given the name of Kanzakura, or Holy Cherry, and it is in honour of this tree that the shrine dedicated to the God of Love was built.

Long ago, when the village of Kagami was smaller than it is at present, it had as one of its chief residents a man called Sodayu. Sodayu was one of those men, to be found in most Japanese villages, who with but little work thrive on the work of others and grow richer than most. He bought and he sold their crops, making commission both ways, and before he was middle-aged he was a rich man.

Sodayu was a widower; but he had a lovely daughter who was aged seventeen, and it was thought by Sodayu that the time had now arrived for him to look about for a desirable husband for Hanano. Accordingly he called her to him and said:

'The time has come, my dear child, when it is my duty to find you a suitable husband. When I have done so you will, I trust, approve of him, for it will be your duty to marry him.'

Of course, O Hanano bowed her willingness to do just as her father decreed; but at the same time she confided in her favourite servant Yuka that she did not care about being married to a man that she might not love.

'What can I do—what would you advise me to do—my dear O Yuka? Do try and think how you can help me to obtain a man I can love. A handsome man he must be, and not more than twenty-two years of age.'

O Yuka answered that the advice asked for was difficult to give; but there was one thing, she said. 'You can go to the temple and pray at the shrine of Musubi-no-Kami, the God of Love. Pray him that the husband your father finds may be handsome and after your own heart. They say that if you pray at this shrine twenty-one days in succession you will obtain the kind of lover you want.'

O Hanano was pleased with the idea, and that afternoon, accompanied by Yuka, her maid, she went to pray at the shrine of Musubi-no-Kami. Day after day they continued until the twenty-first and last day of the series had arrived. They had finished their prayers and were on their way from the temple and passing under the great cherry tree known as the 'Kanzakura' or Holy Cherry, when they saw, standing near its stem, a youth of some twenty or twenty-one years. He was handsome, with a pale face and expressive eyes. In his hand he held a branch of cherry-blossom. He smiled pleasantly at Hanano, and she at him; then, bowing, he came forward and smilingly presented her with the blossom. Hanano blushed, and took the flowers. The youth bowed again and walked away; as did Hanano, who had a fluttering heart and felt very happy, for she thought that this youth must be the one sent by the God of Love in answer to her prayers. 'Of course it must be,' she said to O Yuka. This is the twenty-first, and that completes the course of prayer you spoke of. Am I not lucky? And is he not handsome? I do not think it possible that a more handsome youth was ever seen. I wish he had not gone away so soon.' This and much more did O Hanano prattle to her maid on their way home, upon reaching which the first thing she did was to put the cherry-blossom branch into a vase in her own room.

'O Yuka!' she called for the twentieth time at least. 'Now you must go and find out all you can about the young man; but say nothing to my father as yet. Possibly it is not the husband he is choosing for me; but I can love no other, at all events, and I must love him in secret if this is the case. Now go, dear Yuka. Find out all you can and you will prove yourself more faithful and dear to me than ever.' And the faithful maid went on her young mistress's errand.

Now, O Yuka found out nothing about the youth they had seen under the Holy Cherry tree; but she found out that there was another youth in the village who had fallen greatly in love with her mistress, and, as he had heard that O Hanano's father was looking out for a suitable husband, he intended to apply next day himself. His name was Tokunosuke. He was a fairly well-connected youth, and had some means; but his looks were in no way comparable with those of the youth who had handed the cherry branch to Hanano. Having discovered this much, Yuka returned to her young mistress and reported.

Next day, early in the morning, at the most formal calling hour, Tokunosuke went by appointment to see Hanano's father. Hanano was called to serve tea, and saw the young man. Tokunosuke was scrupulously formal and polite to her, and she to him; and soon after he left Hanano was told by her father that that was the young man whom he had chosen to be her husband. 'He is desirable in every way,' he added. 'He has money. His father is my friend, and he has secretly loved you for some months. You can ask for nothing better.'

O Hanano made no answer, but burst out crying and left the room; and Yuka was called in her stead.

'I have found a most desirable young man as husband for your mistress,' said Sodayu; 'but instead of showing pleasure and gratitude she has flown from the room crying. Can you explain to me the reason? You must know her secrets. Has she a lover unknown to me?'

O Yuka was not prepared to face the anger of her mistress' father, and she thought that truth in this especial instance would further Hanano's interests best. So she told the story faithfully and boldly. Sodayu thanked her for it, and again called his daughter to him, telling her that she must either produce her lover or allow Tokunosuke to call and press his suit. Next morning Tokunosuke did call; but Hanano told him with tears in her eyes that she could not love him, for she loved another, whose name she did not even know herself.

'This is a strange piece of news,' thought Tokunosuke to himself. 'Almost insulting to love a man whose name she does not know!' And, bowing low, he left the house, determined to find out who his nameless rival was, even if he had to disguise himself and follow Hanano to do so.

That very afternoon Hanano and Yuka went to pray as usual, and on coming away they again found the handsome youth standing under the cherry tree, and again he advanced and smilingly handed Hanano a branch full of bloom; but again no words came from his lips, and it was evident to Tokunosuke (who was hiding behind some stone lanterns) that they could not have known each other long.

In a few moments they bowed and separated. O Hanano and her maid walked away from the temple, while the youth under the cherry tree looked after them.

Tokunosuke was now furiously jealous. He came from his hiding-place, and accosted the youth under the cherry tree in a rude and rough tone.

'Who are you, you hateful rascal? Give me your name and address at once! And tell me how you dare tempt the beautiful O Hanano San to love you!' He was about to seize his enemy by the arm when the enemy jumped suddenly back a step, and before Tokunosuke had time to catch him a sudden gust of wind blew the bloom thickly off the cherry tree. So thick and quickly did the blossoms fall, they blinded Tokunosuke for some moments. When he could see again the handsome youth was gone; but there was a strange moaning sound inside the cherry tree, while one of the temple priests came rushing at him in great anger, crying 'Ah! you sacrilegious villain!

What do you mean by attempting violence here? Do you not know that this cherry tree has stood here for hundreds of years? It is sacred, and contains a holy spirit, which sometimes comes forth in the form of a youth. It is he that you tried to touch with your filthy and unholy hand. Begone, I say, and never dare enter this temple again!'

Tokunosuke did not want pressing. He took to his heels and ran, and he ran straight to the house of Sodayu, and told what he had seen, and what had befallen himself, omitting nothing, even to the names the priest had called him.

'Perhaps now your daughter may consent to marry me,' he finished by saying. 'She cannot marry a holy spirit!'

O Hanano was called, and told the story, and was very much upset that the face to whom she had given her heart was that of a spirit. 'What sin have I committed,' she cried, 'falling in love with a God?' And she rushed off to implore forgiveness at the shrine. Long and earnestly she prayed that her sin might be forgiven her. She resolved to devote the rest of her life to the temple, and as she refused to marry she obtained her father's consent. Then she applied for permission to live in the temple and become one of its caretakers. She shaved her head, wore a white linen coat and the crimson pantaloons which denote that you are no longer of the world. O Hanano remained in the temple for the rest of her life, sweeping the grounds, and praying.

The temple still stands. It is highly probable that if the stump of the cherry tree remains another tree is planted beside it, as is usual.

Taken from *Ancient Tales and Folklore of Japan*, by Richard Gordon Smith. London, A. & C. Black [1918]. Scanned, proofed and formatted at sacred-texts.com, February 2006, by John Bruno Hare. This text is in the public domain in the United States because it was published prior to 1923.

Yosoji's Camellia Tree

IN the reign of the Emperor Sanjo began a particularly unlucky time. It was about the year 1013 A. D. when Sanjo came to the throne—the first year of Chowa. Plague broke out. Two years later the Royal Palace was burned down, and a war began with Korea, then known as 'Shiragi.'

In 1016 another fire broke out in the new Palace. A year later the Emperor gave up the throne, owing to blindness and for other causes. He handed over the reins of office to Prince Atsuhara, who was called the Emperor Go Ichijo, and came to the throne in the first year of Kwannin, about 1017 or 1018. The period during which the Emperor Go Ichijo reigned—about twenty years, up to 1036—was one of the worst in Japanese history. There were more wars, more fires, and worse plagues than ever. Things were in disorder generally, and even Kyoto was hardly safe to people of means, owing to the bands of brigands. In 1025 the most appalling outbreak of smallpox came; there was hardly a village or a town in Japan which escaped.

It is at this period that our story begins. Our heroine (if such she may be called) is no less a deity than the Goddess of the Great Mountain of Fuji, which nearly all the world has heard of, or seen depicted. Therefore, if the legend sounds stupid and childish, blame only my way of telling it (simply, as it was told to me), and think of the Great Mountain of Japan, as to which anything should be interesting; moreover, challenge others for a better. I have been able to find none myself.

During the terrible scourge of smallpox there was a village in Suruga Province called Kamiide, which still exists, but is of little importance. It suffered more badly than most other villages. Scarce an inhabitant escaped. A youth of sixteen or seventeen years was much tried. His mother was taken with the disease, and, his father being dead, the responsibility of the household fell on Yosoji—for such was his name.

Yosoji procured all the help he could for his mother, sparing nothing in the way of medicines and attendance; but his mother grew worse day by day, until at last her life was utterly despaired of. Having no other resource left to him, Yosoji resolved to consult a famous fortune-teller and magician, Kamo Yamakiko.

Kamo Yamakiko told Yosoji that there was but one chance that his mother could be cured, and that lay much with his own courage. 'If,' said the fortune-teller, 'you will go to a small brook which flows from the southwestern side of Mount Fuji, and find a small shrine near its source, where Oki-naga-suku-neo 1 is worshipped, you may be able to cure your mother by bringing her water therefrom to drink. But I warn you that the place is full of dangers from wild beasts and other things, and that you may not return at all or even reach the place.'

Yosoji, in no way discouraged, made his mind up that he would start on the following morning, and, thanking the fortune-teller, went home to prepare for an early start.

At three o'clock next morning he was off.

It was a long and rough walk, one which he had never taken before; but he trudged gaily on, being sound of limb and bent on an errand of deepest concern.

Towards midday Yosoji arrived at a place where three rough paths met, and was sorely puzzled which to take. While he was deliberating the figure of a beautiful girl clad in white came towards him through the forest. At first Yosoji felt inclined to run; but the figure called to him in silvery notes, saying:

'Do not go. I know what you are here for. You are a brave lad and a faithful son. I will be your guide to the stream, and—take my word for it—its waters will cure your mother. Follow me if you will, and have no fear, though the road is bad and dangerous.'

The girl turned, and Yosoji followed in wonderment.

In silence the two went for fully four miles, always upwards and into deeper and more gloomy forests. At last a small shrine was reached, in front of which were two Torii's, and from a cleft of a rock gurgled a silvery stream, the clearness of which was such as Yosoji had never seen before.

'There,' said the white-robed girl, 'is the stream of which you are in search. Fill your gourd, and drink of it yourself, for the waters will prevent you catching the plague. Make haste, for it grows late, and it would not be well for you to be here at night. I shall guide you back to the place where I met you.'

Yosoji did as he was bid, drinking, and then filling the bottle to the brim.

Much faster did they return than they had come, for the way was all downhill. On reaching the meeting of the three paths Yosoji bowed low to his guide, and thanked her for her great kindness; and the girl told him again that it was her pleasure to help so dutiful a son.

'In three days you will want more water for your mother,' said she, 'and I shall be at the same place to be your guide again.'

'May I not ask to whom I am indebted for this great kindness?' asked Yosoji.

'No: you must not ask, for I should not tell you,' answered the girl. Bowing again, Yosoji proceeded on his way as fast as he could, wondering greatly.

On reaching home he found his mother worse. He gave her a cup of the water, and told her of his adventures. During the night Yosoji awoke as usual to attend to his mother's wants, and to give her another bowl of water. Next morning he found that she was decidedly better. During the day he gave her three more doses, and on the morning of the third day he set forth to keep his appointment with the fair lady in white, whom he found seated waiting for him on a rock at the meeting of the three paths.

'Your mother is better I can see from your happy face,' said she. 'Now follow me as before, and make haste. Come again in three days, and I will meet you. It will take five trips in all, for the water must be taken fresh. You may give some to the sick villagers as well.'

Five times did Yosoji take the trip. At the end of the fifth his mother was perfectly well, and must thankful for her restoration; besides which, most of the villagers who had not died were cured. Yosoji was the hero of the hour. Every one marvelled, and wondered who the white-robed girl was; for, though they had heard of the shrine of Oki-naga-suku-neo, none of them knew where it was, and but few would have dared to go if they had known. Of course, all knew that Yosoji was indebted in the first place to the fortune-teller Kamo Yamakiko, to whom the whole village sent presents. Yosoji was not easy in his mind. In spite of the good he had brought about, he thought to himself that he owed the whole of his success in finding and bringing the water to the village to his fair guide, and he did not feel that he had shown sufficient gratitude. Always he had hurried home as soon as he had got the precious water, bowing his thanks. That was all, and now he felt as if more were due. Surely prayers at the shrine were due, or something; and who was the lady in white? He must find out. Curiosity called upon him to do so. Thus Yosoji resolved to pay one more visit to the spring, and started early in the morning.

Now familiar with the road, he did not stop at the meeting of the three paths, but pursued his way directly to the shrine. It was the first time he had travelled the road alone, and in spite of himself he felt afraid, though he could not say why. Perhaps it was the oppressive gloom of the mysterious dark forest, overshadowed by the holy mountain of Fuji, which in itself was more mysterious still, and filled one both with superstitious and religious feelings and a feeling of awe as well. No one of any imagination can approach the mountain even to-day without having one or all of these emotions.

Yosoji, however, sped on, as fast as he could go, and arrived at the shrine of Oki-naga-suku-neo. He found that the stream had dried up. There was not a drop of water left. Yosoji flung himself upon his knees before the shrine and thanked the God of Long Breath that he had been the means of curing his mother and the surviving villagers. He prayed that his guide to the spring might reveal her presence, and that he might be enabled to meet her once more to thank her for her kindness. When he arose Yosoji saw his guide standing beside him, and bowed low. She was the first to speak.

'You must not come here,' she said. 'I have told you so before. It is a place of great danger for you. Your mother and the villagers are cured. There is no reason for you to come here more.'

'I have come,' answered Yosoji, 'because I have not fully spoken

my thanks, and because I wish to tell you how deeply grateful I am to you, as is my mother and as are the whole of our villagers. Moreover, they all as well as I wish to know to whom they are indebted for my guidance to the spring. Though Kamo Yamakiko told me of the spring, I should never have found it but for your kindness, which has now extended over five weeks. Surely you will let us know to whom we are so much indebted, so that we may at least erect a shrine in our temple?'

'All that you ask is unnecessary. I am glad that you are grateful. I knew that one so truly filial as you must be so, and it is because of your filial piety and goodness that I guided you to this health-giving spring, which, as you see, is dry, having at present no further use. It is unnecessary that you should know who I am. We must now part: so farewell. End your life as you have begun it, and you shall be happy.' The beautiful maiden swung a wild camellia branch over her head as if with a beckoning motion, and a cloud came down from the top of the Mount Fuji, enveloping her at first in mist. It then arose, showing her figure to the weeping Yosoji, who now began to realize that he loved the departing figure, and that it was no less a figure than that of the Great Goddess of Fujiyama. Yosoji fell on his knees and prayed to her, and the Goddess, acknowledging his prayer, threw down the branch of wild camellia.

Yosoji carried it home, and planted it, caring for it with the utmost attention. The branch grew to a tree with marvellous rapidity, being over twenty feet high in two years. A shrine was built; people came to worship the tree; and it is said that the dewdrops from its leaves are a cure for all eye-complaints.

Taken from *Ancient Tales and Folklore of Japan*, by Richard Gordon

Smith. London, A. & C. Black [1918]. Scanned, proofed and formatted at sacred-texts.com, February 2006, by John Bruno Hare. This text is in the public domain in the United States because it was published prior to 1923.

Both the above stories taken from this anthology are set in a well-defined time and place, instead of 'once upon a time', and are thus examples of magical realist tales. Smith does not try to dress up the language or narrative for Westerners, or sentimentalize the stories, and this is what makes them so appealing.

The style of storytelling most frequently employed in both shamanic stories and in fairy tales is that of magic realism, in which although "the point of departure is 'realistic' (recognizable events in chronological succession, everyday atmosphere, verisimilitude, characters with more or less predictable psychological reactions), … soon strange discontinuities or gaps appear in the 'normal,' true-to-life texture of the narrative" (Calinescu, 1978, p.386). In other words, what happens is that our expectations based on our intuitive knowledge of physics are ultimately breached and knocked out.

Reference

Calinescu, M. (1978) 'The Disguises of Miracle: Notes on Mircea Eliade's Fiction.' In Bryan Rennie (ed.) (2006) *Mircea Eliade: A Critical Reader*, London: Equinox Publishing Ltd.

Who is Lilith for you?

L ilith, according to Hebrew tradition preserved in the Talmud, was the demon lover of Adam, and was immortalized in a sonnet by Dante Gabriel Rossetti:

Of Adam's first wife Lilith, it is told
(The witch he loved before the gift of Eve)
That, ere the snake's, her sweet tongue could deceive,
And her enchanted hair was the first gold.
And still she sits, young while the Earth is old,
And, subtly of herself contemplative,
Draws men to watch the bright web she can weave,
Till heart and body and life are in its hold.
The rose and poppy are her flowers; for where
Is he not found, O Lilith, whom shed scent
And soft shed kisses and soft sleep shall snare?
Lo! as that youth's eyes burned at thine, so went
Thy spell through him, and left his straight neck bent
And round his heart one strangling golden hair.
(*Collected Works*, 216)

There is also a painting by Rossetti of Lady Lilith, dated 1866, now in Delaware Art Museum, Wilmington, Delaware. Symbols appearing in the painting allude to her "femme fatale" reputation: poppies (death and cold) and white roses (sterile passion). However, the representation below, which is in the public domain, was painted by John Collier.

Lilith (1892) by John Collier
in Southport Atkinson Art Gallery

Browning is another poet to write on the subject of Lilith, but his portrayal is very different from that of Rossetti. His poem is almost a positive version of Lilith.

Adam, Lilith and Eve
One day, it thundered and lightened.
Two women, fairly frightened,
Sank to their knees, transformed, transfixed,
At the feet of the man who sat betwixt;
And "Mercy!" cried each—"if I tell the truth
Of a passage in my youth!"
Said This: "Do you mind the morning
I met your love with scorning?
As the worst of the venom left my lips,
I thought, 'If, despite this lie he strips
The mask from my soul with a kiss—I crawl
His slave,—soul, body, and all!'"
Said That: "We stood to be married;
The priest, or some one, tarried;
'If Paradise-door prove locked?' smiled you.
I thought, as I nodded, smiling too,
'Did one, that's away, arrive—nor late
Nor soon should unlock Hell's gate!'"
It ceased to lighten and thunder.
Up started both in wonder,
Looked round and saw that the sky was clear,
Then laughed "Confess you believed us, Dear!"
"I saw through the joke!" the man replied
They re-seated themselves beside.

SHAPE-SHIFTERS AND THEIR STORIES 161

In Browning's poem, first published in 1883, there is more of a focus on Lilith's emotional attributes, rather than that of her ancient demon predecessors. He depicts Lilith and Eve as being friendly and complicitous with each other, as they sit together on either side of Adam. Under the threat of death, Eve admits that she never loved Adam, while Lilith confesses that she always loved him.

In Jewish folklore, from the 8th–10th centuries Alphabet of Ben Sira onwards, Lilith becomes Adam's first wife, who was created at the same time and from the same earth as Adam. This contrasts with Eve, who was created from one of Adam's ribs. The legend was developed further during the Middle Ages, in the tradition of Aggadic midrashim, the Zohar and Jewish mysticism. In the 13th century writings of Rabbi Isaac ben Jacob ha-Cohen, for example, Lilith left Adam because she refused to become subservient to him and then would not return to the Garden of Eden after she mated with archangel Samael. The resulting Lilith legend is still commonly used as source material in modern Western culture, literature, occultism, fantasy, and horror.

The rabbinical myths of Lilith being Adam's first wife seem to relate to the Sumero-Babylonian Goddess Belit-ili, or Belili. To the Canaanites, Lilith was Baalat, the "Divine Lady," and on a tablet from Ur, ca. 2000 BCE, she was addressed as Lillake.

One story is that God created Adam and Lilith as twins joined together at the back. She demanded equality with Adam, but failing to achieve it, she left him in anger. This is sometimes accompanied by a Muslim legend that after leaving Adam Lilith slept with Satan, thus creating the demonic Djinn.

It has even been suggested that perhaps there was a connection between Lilith and the Etruscan divinity Lenith, who possessed no face and waited at the gate of the Underworld along with Eita and Persipnei (Hecate and Persephone) to receive the souls of the dead. The Underworld gate was a yoni, and also a lily, which had "no face." Admission into the Underworld was frequently mythologized as a sexual union. The lily or lilu (lotus) was the Great Mother's flower-yoni, whose title formed Lilith's name.

Even though most of the Lilith legend is derived from Jewish folklore, descriptions of the Lilith demon appear in Iranian, Babylonian, Mexican, Greek, Arab, English, German, Oriental and Native American legends. Also, she has sometimes been associated with legendary and mythological characters such as the Queen of Sheba and Helen of Troy. In medieval Europe she was proclaimed to be the wife, concubine or grandmother of Satan.

As for references to Lilith in "the Old Religion", she appears as a succubus in Aleister Crowley's De Arte Magica, and was one of the middle names of Crowley's first child, Nuit Ma Ahathoor Hecate Sappho Jezebel Lilith Crowley (b. 1904, d.1906). Lilith is also sometimes identified with Babalon in Thelemic writings. Many early occult writers that contributed to modern day Wicca expressed special reverence for Lilith. Charles Leland, for example, associated Aradia with Lilith: Aradia, says Leland, is Herodias, who was regarded in stregheria folklore as being associated with Diana as chief of the witches.

Gerald Gardner asserted that there was continuous historical worship of Lilith to the present day, and that her name is sometimes given to the Goddess being personified in the coven, by the priestess. This idea was further attested by Doreen Valiente, who cited her as a presiding Goddess of the Craft: "the personification of erotic dreams, the suppressed desire for delights". In some contemporary concepts, Lilith is viewed as the embodiment of the Goddess, a designation that is thought to be shared with what these faiths believe to be her counterparts: Inanna, Ishtar, Asherah, Anath and Isis. Another view that has been put forward is that Lilith was originally a Sumerian, Babylonian, or Hebrew Mother Goddess of childbirth, children, women, and sexuality who later became demonized due to the rise of patriarchy. Others hold that Lilith is a dark Moon Goddess on par with the Hindu Kali.

The Western Mystery Tradition associates Lilith with the Klipoth of Kabbalah. Samael Aun Weor in *The Pistis Sophia Unveiled* writes that homosexuals are the "henchmen of Lilith". Likewise, women who undergo wilful abortion, and those who support this practice are "seen in the sphere of Lilith". Dion Fortune writes, "The Virgin Mary is reflected in Lilith", and that Lilith is also the source of "lustful dreams".

Another view that has been proposed is that Lilith is in fact related to a class of female demons Lîlîʔu in Mesopotamian texts. Whatever Lilith's true origins might be though, for there are many different theories and none can be convincingly substantiated, the Lilith in the poem below is the archetypal temptress – a demon who shape-shifts into a beauty to get what she is after:

Lilith in the Heat of the Night
Half a man I am without you
And lust controls my every thought and move
But each time I try to break free
The deeper into the trap I seem to fall
Your beauty so enticed me
I could not pass it by

And now the price I pay for it
You plague upon my life
Lilith in the Cold Light of Day
When young, there can be no denying it,
Your powers held sway over me
But now as age creeps in
They have long since faded and I am released
So try as you might, one last time,
To cast your web of trickery upon me
Your efforts are in vain
And I just laugh in your face

Bibliography

Aun Weor, Samael. *Pistis Sophia Unveiled*, Google Books. p.339

Buckland, Raymond. *The Witch Book*, Visible Ink Press, November 1, 2001.

Fortune, Dion. *Psychic Self-Defence*, Google books. pp. 126–128.

Hurwitz, Siegmund. *Lilith, die erste Eva: eine Studie uber dunkle Aspekte des Wieblichen. Zurich*: Daimon Verlag, 1980, 1993. English tr. *Lilith, the First Eve: Historical and Psychological Aspects of the Dark Feminine*, translated by Gela Jacobson. Einsiedeln, Switzerland: Daimon Verlag, 1992 ISBN 3-85630-545-9."Excerpts from Lilith-The first Eve".

Leland, Charles. *Aradia Gospel of the Witches*, EZreads Publications, LLC (24 Feb 2009)

Grimassi, Raven. *Italian Witchcraft: The Old Religion of Southern Europe*, Llewellyn Publications, U.S. (2000)

Valiente, Doreen, "Lilith-The First Eve". Imbolc. 2002.

Hefner, Alan G. "Lilith" http://www.pantheon.org/articles/l/lilith.html [accessed 01/05/2012]

Werewolf Legends

Not all shape-shifting is voluntary. The Werewolf of European folklore is a cursed and tragic figure — as were the were-tigers of India and the leopard and hyena men of Africa. In his *Natural History*, Pliny recounts (somewhat sceptically) this tale of the Antaei in Arcadia: each year one man is chosen by lot and taken to the shores of a sacred lake. His clothes are removed, hung on an oak, and he swims to the woods on the lake's other side. He then runs wild with the wolves, half-forgetting his human kin. But if he manages to refrain from eating human flesh for a full nine years he may cross the lake, put on his clothes, and regain man-shape again. In medieval Christian legendry, St. Natalis cursed the people of Ossory, who all became wolves for seven long years. A priest met one of the penitent sinners, a wolf who addressed him in human speech, imploring him to please come quickly and shrive his dying wolf-wife. Another example can be found in a French tale that concerns a woman who buys a green belt from an odd-looking pedlar. Her husband forbids her to wear the thing, but she cannot resist the belt's strange appeal. Once on, it will not come off again, and the poor woman becomes a wolf every night for the next seven years. The tale chosen for inclusion in the volume though, is *The Lay of the Werewolf* by Marie de France.

Of the personal history of Marie de France very little is known. The date and place of her birth are still matters for conjecture, and until comparatively recent times literary antiquaries were doubtful even as to which century she flourished in. In the epilogue to her Fables she states that she is a native of the Ile-de-France, but despite this she is believed to have been of Norman origin, and also to have lived the greater part of her life in England. Her work, which holds few suggestions of Anglo-Norman forms of thought or expression, was written in a literary dialect that in all likelihood was widely estranged from the common Norman tongue, and from this (though the manuscripts in which they are preserved are dated later) we may judge her poems to have been composed in the second half of the twelfth century. The prologue of her Lais contains a dedication to some unnamed king, and her Fables are inscribed to a certain Count William, circumstances which are held by some to prove that she was of noble origin and not merely a trouvère from necessity.

The Lay of the Werewolf

In the long ago there dwelt in Brittany a worshipful baron, for whom the king of that land had a warm affection, and who was happy in the esteem of his peers and the love of his beautiful wife.

One only grief had his wife in her married life, and that was the mysterious absence of her husband for three days in every week. Where he disappeared to neither she nor any member of her household knew. These excursions preyed upon her mind, so that at last she resolved to challenge him regarding them.

"Husband," she said to him pleadingly one day after he had just returned from one of these absences, "I have something to ask of you, but I fear that my request may vex you, and for this reason I hesitate to make it." The baron took her in his arms and, kissing her tenderly bade her state her request, which he assured her would by no means vex him.

"It is this," she said, "that you will trust me sufficiently to tell me where you spend those days when you are absent from me. So fearful have I become regarding these withdrawals and all the mystery that enshrouds them that I know neither rest nor comfort; indeed, so distraught am I at times that I feel I shall die for very anxiety. Oh, husband, tell me where you go and why you tarry so long!"

In great agitation the husband put his wife away from him, not daring to meet the glance of her imploring, anxious eyes.

"For the mercy of God, do not ask this of me," he besought her. "No good could come of your knowing, only great and terrible evil. Knowledge would mean the death of your love for me, and my everlasting desolation."

"You are jesting with me, husband," she replied; "but it is a cruel jest. I am all seriousness, I do assure you. Peace of mind can never be mine until my question is fully answered."

But the baron, still greatly perturbed, remained firm. He could not tell her, and she must rest content with that. The lady, however, continued to plead, sometimes with tenderness, more often with tears and heart-piercing reproaches, until at length the baron, trusting to her love, decided to tell her his secret.

"I have to leave you because periodically I become a bisclaveret," he said. ('Bisclaveret' is the Breton name for Werewolf.) "I hide myself in the depths of the forest, live on wild animals and roots, and go unclad as any beast of the field."

When the lady had recovered from the horror of this disclosure and had rallied her senses to her aid, she turned to him again, determined at any cost to learn all the circumstances connected with this terrible transformation.

"You know that I love you better than all the world, my husband," she began; "that never in our life together have I done aught to forfeit your love or your trust. So do, I beseech you, tell me all—tell me where you hide your clothing before you become a Werewolf?"

"That I dare not do, dear wife," he replied, "for if I should lose my raiment or even be seen quitting it I must remain a Werewolf so long as I live. Never again could I become a man unless my garments were restored to me.

"Then you no longer trust me, no longer love me?" she cried. "Alas, alas that I have forfeited your confidence! Oh that I should live to see such a day!"

Her weeping broke out afresh, this time more piteously than before. The baron, deeply touched, and willing by any means to alleviate her distress, at last divulged the vital secret which he had held from her so long.

But from that hour his wife cast about for ways and means to rid herself of her strange husband, of whom she now went in exceeding fear. In course of time she remembered a knight of that country who had long sought her love, but whom she had repulsed. To him she appealed, and right gladly and willingly he pledged himself to aid her. She showed him where her lord concealed his clothing, and begged him to spoil the Werewolf of his vesture on the next occasion on which he set out to assume his transformation. The fatal period soon returned. The baron disappeared as usual, but this time he did not return to his home. For days friends, neighbours, and menials sought him diligently, but no trace of him was to be found, and when a year had elapsed the search was at length abandoned, and the lady was wedded to her knight.

Some months later the king was hunting in the great forest near the missing baron's castle. The hounds, unleashed, came upon the scent of a wolf, and pressed the animal hard. For many hours they pursued him, and when about to seize him, Bisclaveret—for it was he—turned with such a human gesture of despair to the king, who had ridden hard upon his track, that the royal huntsman was moved to pity. To the king's surprise the Werewolf placed its paws together as if in supplication, and its great jaws moved as if in speech.

"Call off the hounds," cried the monarch to his attendants. "This quarry we will take alive to our palace. It is too marvellous a thing to be killed."

Accordingly they returned to the court, where the Werewolf became an object of the greatest curiosity to all. So frolicsome yet so gentle was he that he became a universal favourite. At night he slept in the king's room, and by day he followed him with all the dumb faithfulness of a dog. The king was extremely attached to him, and never permitted his shaggy favourite to be absent from his side for a moment.

One day the monarch held a high court, to which his great vassals and barons and all the lords of his broad demesnes were bidden. Among them came the knight who had wed the wife of Bisclaveret. Immediately upon sight of him the Werewolf flew at him with a savage joy that astonished those accustomed to his usual gentleness and docility. So fierce was the attack that the knight would have been killed had not the king intervened to save him. Later, in the royal hunting-lodge she who had been the wife of Bisclaveret came to offer the king a rich present. When he saw her, the animal's rage knew no bounds, and despite all restraint he succeeded in mutilating her fair face in the most frightful manner. But for a certain wise counsellor this act would have cost Bisclaveret his life. This sagacious person, who knew of the animal's customary docility, insisted that some evil must have been done him.

"There must be some reason why this beast holds these twain in such mortal hate," he said. "Let this woman and her husband be brought hither so that they may be straightly questioned. She was once the wife of one who was near to your heart, and many marvellous happenings have ere this come out of Brittany."

The king hearkened to this sage counsel, for he loved the Werewolf, and was loath to have him slain. Under pressure of examination Bisclaveret's treacherous wife confessed all that she had done, adding that in her heart she believed the king's favourite animal to be no other than her former husband.

Instantly on learning this, the king demanded the Werewolf's vesture from the treacherous knight her lover, and when this was brought to him he caused it to be spread before the wolf. But the animal behaved as though he did not see the garments.

Then the wise counsellor again came to his aid.

"You must take the beast to your own secret chamber, sire," he told the king; "for not without great shame and tribulation can he become a man once more, and this he dare not suffer in the sight of all."

This advice the king promptly followed, and when after some little time he, with two lords of his fellowship in attendance, re-entered the secret chamber, he found the wolf gone, and the baron so well beloved asleep in his bed.

With great joy and affection the king aroused his friend, and when the baron's feelings permitted him he related his adventures. As soon as his master had heard him out he not only restored to him all that had been taken from him, but added gifts the number and richness of which rendered him more wealthy and important than ever, while in just anger he banished from his realm the wife who had betrayed her lord, together with her lover.

The Werewolf Superstition

The Werewolf superstition is, or was, as prevalent in Brittany as in other parts of France and Europe. The term 'Werewolf' literally means 'man-wolf', and was applied to a man supposed to be temporarily or permanently transformed into a wolf. In its origins the belief may have been a phase of lycanthropy, a disease in which the sufferer imagines himself to have been transformed into an animal, and in ancient and medieval times of very frequent occurrence. It may, on the other hand, be a relic of early cannibalism. Communities of semi-civilized people would begin to shun those who devoured human flesh, and they would in time be ostracized and classed with wild beasts, the idea that they had something in common with these would grow, and the belief that they were able to transform themselves into veritable animals would be likely to arise therefrom.

There were two kinds of Werewolf, voluntary and involuntary. The voluntary included those persons who because of their taste for human flesh had withdrawn from intercourse with their fellows, and who appeared to possess a certain amount of magical power, or at least sufficient to permit them to transform themselves into animal shape at will. This they effected by merely disrobing, by taking off a girdle made of human skin, or putting on a similar belt of wolf-skin (obviously a later substitute for an entire wolf-skin; in some cases we hear of their donning the skin entire). In other instances the body was rubbed with magic ointment, or rain-water was drunk out of a wolf's footprint. The brains of the animal were also eaten. Olaus

The Were-wolf

Magnus says that the werewolves of Livonia drained a cup of beer on initiation, and repeated certain magical words. In order to throw off the wolf-shape the animal girdle was removed, or else the magician merely muttered certain formulae. In some instances the transformation was supposed to be the work of Satan.

The superstition regarding werewolves seems to have been exceedingly prevalent in France during the sixteenth century, and there is evidence of numerous trials of persons accused of Werewolfism, in some of which it was clearly shown that murder and cannibalism had taken place. Self-hallucintion was accountable for many of the cases, the supposed werewolves declaring that they had transformed themselves and had slain many people. But about the beginning of the seventeenth century native common sense came to the rescue, and such confessions were not credited. In Teutonic and Slavonic countries it was complained by men of learning that the werewolves did more damage than real wild animals, and the existence of a regular 'college' or institution for the practice of the art of animal transformation among werewolves was affirmed.

Involuntary werewolves, of which class Bisclaveret was evidently a member, were often persons transformed into animal shape because of the commission of sin, and condemned to pass a certain number of years in that form. Thus certain saints metamorphosed sinners into wolves. In Armenia it was thought that a sinful woman was condemned to pass seven years in the form of a wolf. To such a woman a demon appeared, bringing a wolf-skin. He commanded her to don it, and from that moment she became a wolf, with all the nature of the wild beast, devouring her own children and those of strangers, and wandering forth at night, undeterred by locks, bolts, or bars, returning only with the morning to resume her human form.

It was, of course, in Europe, where the wolf was one of the largest carnivorous animals, that the Werewolf superstition chiefly gained currency. In Eastern countries, where similar beliefs prevailed, bears, tigers, and other beasts of prey were substituted for the lupine form of colder climes.

Taken from *Legends and Romances of Brittany* by Lewis Spence. New York: Frederick A. Stokes Company Publishers [1917]. Scanned at sacred-texts.com, August, 2004. John Bruno Hare, redactor. This text is in the public domain. These files may be used for any non-commercial purpose, provided this notice of attribution is left intact.

The Dybbuk:
A Shape-shifter,
but with a Difference

According to Jewish folklore, a dybbuk is a disembodied human spirit in search of a living human to possess. In view of the fact such spirits transform themselves into human form this way, they can be regarded as a "species" of shape-shifters too and so worthy of a Chapter of their own in this volume.

As Professor Allan Nadler explains, a dazzling array of demonic ghosts and evil spirits, and a host of laws, customs, formulas, and talismanic devices designed to ward them off, permeate classical rabbinic literature, to say nothing of the Kabbalah.

In late Roman antiquity, the demonic possession of individuals was a belief so widely accepted that the ability to "cast out" was one reason why numbers of Jews in first-century Palestine became convinced that Jesus of Nazareth was their divinely anointed saviour. Such casting-out was, indeed, the very first of Jesus' miracles recorded in the Gospels (Mark 1:23-26). While, for almost a millennium after the Talmudic era, there are no clearly recorded accounts of either possessions or exorcisms, the belief regained prominence with the rise of the Lurianic school of Kabbalah in the mid-16th century.

The Kabbalists of Safed developed elaborate theories about the transmigration of souls, both benevolent and malevolent; in dealing with the latter, they touted the expertise of Rabbi Isaac Luria

Hanna Rovina as Leah'le in *The Dybbuk*, ca. 1920

and his disciples in banishing what came to be known as dybbuks—malevolent, "clinging" spirits from the netherworld. It cannot be entirely coincidental that in both Judaism and Catholicism, a formal liturgy for the rite of exorcism began to develop at around the same time. (The Safed Kabbalists were mostly descendants of Marranos who had lived as Catholics for generations.) But in one major respect, the two faiths differed: while in the Church the competent exorcist can confidently rely on the miraculous efficacy of the rite itself, in Jewish lore the practitioner is called upon to enter into extensive "conversations" and complex negotiations with the evil spirit to convince it to depart. [This is similar to what shamans do in cases of Soul Loss. They enter into negotiations with lost soul parts in attempt to persuade them it is now safe to return again].

This feature … is rooted in the belief that the dybbuk is the restless soul of a sinner whose transgressions in life have barred him (or her) from entry into Gehenna, the transitory station for the expurgation and forgiveness of sins that can ultimately lead to admittance into heaven. Such spirits, caught in a state of limbo, would seek respite by attaching themselves to the souls of living humans with whom they had had some form of intimate contact during their lives….

The complex task of the Jewish exorcist was to identify the dybbuk by name, uncover the nature of its earthly sins, and negotiate acceptable terms for its departure from the body of the possessed person. The Jewish exorcist thus served not only to relieve the suffering of the victim but also to act as an advocate on behalf of the dybbuk itself, usually by assuring it entry into Gehenna and final redemption (Nadler, 2010).

The initial appearance of a dibbuk is in a story included in the Ma'aseh Book,11 which was first published in 1602, and which contains material whose origin is considerably earlier than that date. In this story the spirit which took possession of a young man was the spirit of one who in this life had sinned egregiously, and which could therefore find no peace. It had entered the youth's body after having been forced to flee its previous abode, the body of a cow which was about to be slaughtered. It is this form of the belief, possession by the restless spirit of a deceased person, which gained such popularity in later times. In essence this represents a version of the doctrine of the transmigration of souls, gilgul, which the older Spanish Kabbalah developed. (Trachtenberg, 1939, p.50)

Better known for popularizing the legend of the dybbuk, however, is Isaac Bashevis Singer, 1902 – 1991, a Polish-born, Jewish-American author. He was a leading figure in the Yiddish literary movement and won the Nobel Prize in Literature in 1978. The figure of the dybbuk appears in many of his stories, *The Dead Fiddler*, for example. Singer's dybbuks, like ghosts, can be mischievous, evil, or benevolent, and the characters in his tales often ascribe events in their lives to spirits such as these.

As well as featuring in Isaac Bashevis Singer's stories, the figure of the dybbuk has also provided the inspiration for a play. *The Dybbuk*, or *Between Two Worlds*, written by Shloyme-Zanvel Rapaport (known as Sh. Ansky), became probably the most popular and commercially successful play in the history of the Yiddish and Hebrew theatre.

In addition to its remarkable success with Yiddish audiences all across Eastern Europe, the Hebrew version of the play became the signature performance piece of the Habimah troupe from its Moscow premiere in 1922 through multiple productions over the next decades in Tel Aviv. A film version of the play in Yiddish and translations into more than a dozen other languages amplified its reach still further. The play tells the tragic story of a young Jewish bride who is possessed under her wedding canopy by the spirit of a dead Kabbalist, whose wife she was destined to be through their parents' mutual contract at birth and their own adolescent romance. It culminates in the transmigration of the pained soul of its protagonist, Khonon, a young religious scholar immersed in Kabbalah, into the body of Leah, his beloved. Ansky's inspiration for the drama is known to have been the materials he collected during his ambitious 1912-1913 ethnographic explorations of rural Jewish communities throughout the Ukraine, which among other riches yielded a vast folklore of evil spirits, transmigrated souls, and dybbuks as well as vivid tales of exorcisms performed by great rabbis and Kabbalists.

The setting for the poem below, however, is not the kind of village in Poland that Sh. Ansky or Singer wrote about, but the present-day Jewish enclave of Hendon in North London.

The Dybbuk of Hendon

All the pent-up emotions

So long kept under lock and key

And for so many dutiful years while raising my family

Finally free to express themselves

And I cannot in any way be blamed for my behaviour

As it is the dybbuk who is responsible

Of all the nice Jewish women to choose from

Why pick me though

Esther from Hendon

Did you perhaps decide I needed a break from the strain of conforming to impossibly high ideals

More than others less worthy perhaps

Anyway, whatever the reason, please let me express my gratitude

Through you my petty transgressions

Are no longer unpardonable sins

And I can once again sleep at night

Free from the feelings of guilt

That previously tore me apart

And that is why, in spite of your invasive nature,

I have so much to thank you despite what other members of the community may think

But now the rabbi has been sent for

To curb and suppress all my natural instincts once more

But oh how I have enjoyed this holiday from being who I am expected to be

And even dare to hope I will have the chance to repeat it
some time

Perhaps it could even become an annual event

Though not on Jewish holy days of course

And please remember all of you

I was in no way responsible for what happened, the blot on
my copybook

The dybbuk in me was

And I am once again, and still remain, the model house-
wife I was raised to be

So please stop staring at me like that, as if I were some sort
of outcast

Instead, take the same Esther you knew and loved back
again into your flock

In Jewish folklore, a dybbuk (Yiddish: ãéáå÷, from Hebrew
attachment) is a malicious or malevolent possessing spirit believed to
be the dislocated soul of a dead person. Dybbuks are said to have
escaped from Sheol or to have been turned away for serious
transgressions, such as suicide, for which the soul is denied entry.
The dybbuk attaches itself to the body of a living person and inhabits
the flesh. According to belief, a soul that has been unable to fulfill its
function during its lifetime is given another opportunity to do so in

dybbuk form. It supposedly leaves the host body once it has accomplished its goal, sometimes after being helped.

It has been suggested that scholars are those most at risk of being possessed:

Since all creation is engaged in the quest for perfection, all things striving to attain the next higher degree of being, the demons, too, are perpetually seeking to acquire the body of man, their greatest desire being for that of the scholar, the highest type of human. This is why scholars in particular must be careful not to be out alone at night. (Trachtenberg, 1939, p.50)

However, Trachtenberg's belief that women are more at risk than men of being possessed is fortunately not one that many people these days would share:

But just as woman, in herself imperfect, seeks perfection through union with man, so the demons seek to unite themselves primarily with woman, who represents the next degree of creation above them. This is why women are more prone to sorcery than are men; the sorceress is a woman through whom the demon that has possessed her operates, or one who through close association with demons has acquired their malevolent attributes. (ibid. p.50 & 51).

Many would argue that Jewish history does not have any verifiable accounts of these creatures. Yet surprisingly, references to otherworldly spirits can be found in the Tanakh. The Book of Samuel (18:10) describes a "ruach elohim ra'ah (a bad, or evil, spirit of G-d) that attaches itself to King Saul. Although the spirit is not given a name, its description closely parallels what later becomes referred to as a dybbuk, or spiritual attachment, a ghost, usually sinister, that clings to the soul of a living person.

Although each type of spirit is imbued with its own characteristics, they all represent spirits, or life energies, that have gone astray. The dybbuk is typically characterized as a sinister demon, while the ibbur (meaning impregnation) is most often thought to be its opposite: a spirit that brings about, or helps to facilitate something positive in a person's life.

(The ibbur) is probably the most positive form of possession, and also the most complicated. It happens when a righteous soul decides to occupy a living person's body for a time, and joins, or spiritually "impregnates" the existing soul.

Jews, unlike Catholics, do not believe in the possibility of demonic possession. Instead, they believe that, on very rare occasions, there can be a possession of a living person by the soul of one who has left the body, but not the world, and they're seeking a body to possess to finish whatever they need to finish.

So how does a dybbuk take hold of a person? The dybbuk is drawn to someone whose soul and their body are not fully connected with each other because of severe melancholy or psychosis, for example, when a person is not in balance. It seeks a particular person who in their current lifetime is going through what the possessing spirit went through, and so the possessing spirit is drawn to compatibility — to someone who is struggling with the same problems it did.

You can apparently tell when someone is genuinely the victim of a dybbuk if the person is able to tell you things they would ordinarily not know — like what you dreamed last night, what is happening across the street, maybe they can even speak a different language that they have never known before. If this kind of bad possession takes hold, the solution is believed to be exorcism.

The Jewish exorcism ritual is performed by a rabbi who has mastered practical Kabbalah. The ceremony involves a quorum of 10 people who gather in a circle around the possessed person. The group recites Psalm 91 three times, and the rabbi then blows the shofar — a ram's horn. It is blown in a certain way, with certain notes, in effect to shatter the body, so to speak, so that the soul who possesses the victim will be shaken loose. After it has been shaken loose, it becomes possible to communicate with it and ask it what it is here for. The rabbi can then pray for it and conduct a ceremony to enable it to feel safe and finished so that it can leave the person's body.

The point of the exorcism is to heal both the person being possessed and the spirit doing the possessing. This is a stark contrast to the Catholic exorcism that is intended to drive away the offending spirit or demon.

There is also a positive aspect to a dybbuk. Sometimes a spirit guide will come to a person in a time of need to help. The second kind of possession is called 'sod ha'ibbur', which is Hebrew for 'mystery impregnation.' The spirit of someone who has struggled and overcome what you have struggled with and cannot overcome will be lent to you from the spirit world to possess you, encourage you, and help you to deal with whatever obstacle you are faced with. Then when it is done and you have managed to achieve what you needed to, the spirit guide leaves you and returns to where it came from.

The positive aspect to a dybbuk brings to mind the figure of the wounded healer, an archetype for a shamanizing journey. The apprentice shaman typically undergoes a type of sickness that pushes her or him to the brink of death, and this happens for two reasons:

1. The shaman crosses over to the Underworld. This happens so the shaman can venture to its depths to bring back vital information for the sick, and the tribe.

2. The shaman must become sick to understand sickness. When the shaman overcomes her or his own sickness s/he will hold the cure to heal all that suffer, and this is the uncanny mark of the wounded healer.

Asclepius was an example of a wounded healer, a physician who in identification of his own wounds created a sanctuary at Epidaurus in order to treat others.

References

"Of Devils and Dybbuks" by Allan Nadler http://www.jewishideasdaily.com/content/module/2010/11/30/main-feature/1/of-devils-and-dybbuks

Jewish Magic and Superstition: A Study in Folk Religion by Joshua Trachtenberg. New York: Behrman's Jewish Book House. [1939]. Scanned, proofed and formatted by John Bruno Hare at sacred-texts.com, January 2008. This text is in the public domain in the US because its copyright was not renewed in a timely fashion at the US Copyright office as required by law at the time.

Index

If you enjoyed Shape Shifters you might also like:

Sacred Mountains: Stories of the Mystic Mountains

On the mountains of truth you can never climb in vain: either you will reach a point higher up today, or you will be training your powers so that you will be able to climb higher tomorrow.
~ Friedrich Nietzsche

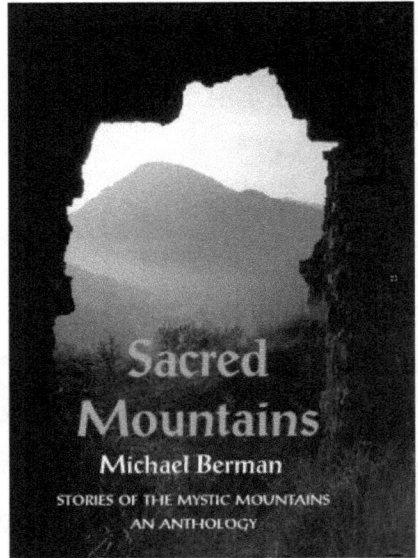

Sacred
Mountains
Michael Berman
STORIES OF THE MYSTIC MOUNTAINS
AN ANTHOLOGY

All the stories presented in this collection contain shamanic elements, so the obvious starting point is to explain what is meant by this. The term 'shaman' is a controversial one. Initially employed by early anthropologists to refer to a specific category of magical practitioners from Siberia, the term is now widely used to denote similar practitioners from a variety of cultures around the world. This application of an originally culture-specific term to a more general usage has caused problems with regard to definition, with disagreements among scholars over whether certain features, such as soul flight or possession, or certain types of altered states of consciousness, should or should not be listed among the core characteristics of shamanism (Wilby, 2011, p.252).

www.ingramcontent.com/pod-product-compliance
Lightning Source LLC
Chambersburg PA
CBHW050651270326
41927CB00012B/2978